★ ★ ★ ★ ★ ★ ★ ★ ★ ★ ★ ★ ★ ★ ★ ★ ★

OUTRAGEOUS WOMEN OF COLONIAL AMERICA

Mary Rodd Furbee

JOSSEY-BASS
A Wiley Imprint
www.josseybass.com

★ ★ ★ ★ ★ ★ ★ ★ ★ ★ ★ ★ ★ ★ ★ ★ ★

Published by Jossey-Bass
A Wiley Imprint
989 Market Street, San Francisco, CA 94103-1741   www.josseybass.com

Published simultaneously in Canada
Illustrations on pp. 15, 23, 32, 90, and 111 copyright ©2001 by Lisa Brown
Maps on pp. x, 50, and 82 copyright ©2001 by Jessica Wolk-Stanley
Designed by BTDnyc

Limit of Liability/Disclaimer of Warranty: While the publisher and author have used their best efforts in preparing this book, they make no representations or warranties with respect to the accuracy or completeness of the contents of this book and specifically disclaim any implied warranties of merchantability or fitness for a particular purpose. No warranty may be created or extended by sales representatives or written sales materials. The advice and strategies contained herein may not be suitable for your situation. You should consult with a professional where appropriate. Neither the publisher nor author shall be liable for any loss of profit or any other commercial damages, including but not limited to special, incidental, consequential, or other damages.

Readers should be aware that Internet Web sites offered as citations and/or sources for further information may have changed or disappeared between the time this was written and when it is read.

Jossey-Bass books and products are available through most bookstores. To contact Jossey-Bass directly call our Customer Care Department within the U.S. at 800-956-7739, outside the U.S. at 317-572-3986, or fax 317-572-4002.

Jossey-Bass also publishes its books in a variety of electronic formats. Some content that appears in print may not be available in electronic books.

Library of Congress Cataloging-in-Publication Data

Furbee, Mary R. (Mary Rodd), 1954–
        Outrageous women of Colonial America / Mary Rodd Furbee.
            p. cm.
        Includes index.
        ISBN 0-471-38299-X (acid-free paper)
            1.United States—History—Colonial period, ca. 1600–1775 Biography—Juvenile literature. 2. Women—United States—Biography—Juvenile literature. [1. Women—Biography. 2. United States—History—Colonial Period, ca.1600–1775.] I. Title
        E187.5.F87 2001
        920. 72'0973'09032—dc21
        [B]

                                                    00–043385

Printed in the United States of America
FIRST EDITION
PB Printing   10 9 8 7 6 5

C O N T E N T S

★ ★ ★ ★ ★ ★ ★ ★ ★ ★

★ ★ ★ ★ ★ ★ ★ ★ ★ ★ ★ ★ ★ ★ ★ ★ ★ ★

PART THREE. THE SOUTH

Courageous Captain John Smith. Honest George Washington. Brainy Thomas Jefferson. You probably know all about these celebrated founding fathers of America. But have you ever stopped to wonder what the women were up to?

Tucked away in your imagination are probably a few homespun images: a matronly woman in a bonnet piecing a patchwork quilt, a backwoods pioneer watching nervously for marauding Native Americans, a patriotic wife boycotting English tea. That's fine, as far as it goes. But why settle for such tame images, when the flesh-and-blood women of colonial America were far more interesting?

The real women of the American colonies were incredibly diverse and dynamic. They were Puritan preachers, eastern aristocrats, native queens, and backwoods settlers. They were English, Scottish, African, and Native American. They were rich and poor, enslaved and free. Some were rebels with a cause; others were loyal to a distant king.

★ ★ ★ ★ ★ ★ ★ ★ ★ ★ ★ ★ ★ ★ ★ ★ ★ ★ ★ ★

Colonial women tilled soil, ran shops, and published newspapers. They were arrested for preaching on the street and hanged for heresy. They wrote propaganda, negotiated peace treaties, and spied against their enemies. They were enterprising, rebellious, and committed! Many behaved in ways women had never dared before. When I first learned all this about our remarkable foremothers, I was surprised—and proud. I think you'll feel the same.

Something else might surprise you, too. Some very famous colonial women don't have their own chapters in this book—such as the celebrated Pocahontas and the camp followers Molly Pitcher and Margaret Corbin. They were important women in their day, but their exploits have been so twisted over time that the truth about their lives has been lost. We all love a good yarn, of course. Legends aren't real history, though, and in this book we're honoring the real McCoy.

The best-known colonial women were wealthy, educated, and from prominent families. An elite minority of women who learned to read and write left behind letters, diaries, and other writings that help us piece together their lives. Unfortunately, we know a lot less about illiterate poor, enslaved, and Native American women. Thanks to a handful of resourceful journalists and family members, however, a few stories about ordinary (yet extraordinary!) women survive.

In colonial times, most women kept house and raised children. Yet many worked for a living, too. Housework, in those days, was a daily grind you can't imagine! Every little thing was made from scratch—soap, butter, cloth, bullets, everything. Also, most women had lots of children, not just two or three. Given that—and the diseases that ran rampant—it's no surprise that the average colonial woman lived to be only 40 years old.

Women in the American colonies also had hardly any rights. They could not vote, own property, or manage their own money. Men held the purse strings and made the decisions. "Good" women obeyed meekly. "Bad" women made waves.

Virtually all women and men in colonial times were religious, and many believed that God meant for men to lord it over inferior females. During this time, however, great religious up-heavals had shattered established churches into dozens of sects. In the 1500s, England's official Church of

Courtesy of the Collection of the New York Historical Society

England—known as the Anglicans—split from the Roman Catholic Church headquartered in Rome, Italy. Then Puritans, Lutherans, Presbyterians, and Quakers split from the Anglicans. Many of these dissenters wound up coming to America to escape persecution for practicing their religions. Most of the new religious leaders were still men, of course, but some women were also inspired to question religious authority.

Along with religious turmoil, a series of wars rocked the colonies from the 1600s to the revolution. The Spanish, French, Portuguese, Dutch, and English fought with each other and with

Native American tribes, over who would control the fertile New World. By 1760, Britain had ousted the other European powers but then discovered it had a new battle on its hands—rebellious American colonists!

In the early colonial years, the first colonists to arrive were British to the bone. Their children, grandchildren, and later descendants were born on American soil—not British—so they felt less loyalty to a far-off country they'd never seen. A fondness for liberty took hold, which stumped the English monarchs and Parliament. In fact, the kings, queens, and Parliament could be real

★ ★ ★ ★ ★ ★ ★ ★ ★ ★ ★ ★ ★ ★ ★ ★ ★ ★

RELIGION IN THE NEW WORLD

The story of religious wars in Europe is long, complicated—and bloody. Catholics persecuted Protestants. Protestants persecuted Catholics. Both persecuted reformers in their own ranks. In the New World, the age-old conflicts continued, but there was plenty of room for people of different sects to get away from each other.

Before the American Revolution, New England's Puritans and Pilgrims (later called Congregationalists) thought that the Catholics of Maryland and the Anglicans of Virginia led unholy lives. In turn, the Anglicans and Catholics considered the Puritans fanatical and rigid. Baptists, Methodists, Presbyterians, and Quakers also thought they alone knew the way to heaven. Many courageous, questioning women, like those in this book, paved the way for a more tolerant America. Fighting a common enemy during the revolution helped unite different faiths and colonies, too.

★ ★ ★ ★ ★ ★ ★ ★ ★ ★ ★ ★ ★ ★ ★ ★ ★ ★

dunderheads when it came to dealing with their "children" in the far-off colonies.

For a long time, Britain left American colonists alone to govern and tax themselves, and to regulate their own trade. Then in the mid-1700s, the mother country started laying down the law. The colonists, an independent breed from the beginning, didn't appreciate this high-handedness. A spirit of rebellion spread like wildfire. Suddenly, men were off fighting a revolution. Suddenly, women were needed to keep the home fires burning—and help win the war.

The war put women through the ringer, but it was exciting and liberating, too. Many women discovered how strong they were in body and spirit. Their husbands and sons died in battle. Their homes burned to the ground, and wood for heating their homes was scarce. So was food. Disease spread into town from unsanitary army camps. All the while, women coped with and overcame these hardships. They grieved and suffered, protected the people they loved, served their cause—and survived!

After discovering their own strengths, many of the women in this book were not about to fade quietly into the woodwork when peace arrived! Abigail Adams kept pestering her husband about women's rights. Deborah Samson shocked many people by giving public lectures about her adventures. Other outrageous women opened and supported schools and colleges for females, where new ideas about the place of women in the world flourished. It took 125 years, but women educated in these schools later led a movement that revolutionized society. Thanks to the pioneering efforts of women of the American colonies, a new generation of outrageous women won the right to vote.

Part One

★ ★ ★ ★ ★ ★ ★ ★ ★ ★

NEW ENGLAND

THE NEW ENGLAND colonies of Massachusetts, Rhode Island, Connecticut, and New Hampshire were founded by Protestant sects from England. Later they were joined by small groups of Catholics and Jews. All came here to worship their own way and build prosperous lives. Enterprising men and women settled in tidy little villages and on family farms. Industries prospered, especially shipbuilding, cod fishing, and trading in furs and slaves. Smaller shops kept busy doing printing, blacksmithing, shoe making, hat making, weaving, and more. Boston, Massachusetts, became New England's major port city.

Anne Marbury Hutchinson

(1 5 9 1 – 1 6 4 3)

Anne Hutchinson came to Boston, Massachusetts, in 1634, to shine a holy beacon of light back on immoral England. She sure didn't expect her own flock of Puritans to label her the greatest sinner in New England!

Born in Alford, England, in 1591, Anne was the oldest of a dozen brothers and sisters. Bossing them around gave her plenty of practice at ruling the roost. Anne's father, Anglican minister Frances Marbury, also taught her how to rebel. At that time, everyone in England was supposed to obey church laws and pay taxes to the official national religion, Anglicanism. Instead, Anne's outspoken father criticized the church and was jailed twice for doing so.

When Anne was 14, a joyous event took place: Her father got out of prison! Not only that, the forgiving Anglicans gave him back his minister's robes and assigned him to a London church. Bustling London, 125 miles from sleepy Alford, widened Anne's sheltered eyes! Everywhere she turned she saw fabulous mansions, packed

Courtesy of Bettmann/Corbis

theaters, and shops full of fancy goods. Anne also noticed that some of the women in glittering jewels, powdered hair, and low-cut necklines kicked the barefoot beggars lying in the gutters. Many of the gentlemen and merchants in stiff colors and gaudy wigs also gambled to excess and kept mistresses. Like her father, Anne thought these sinners were leading society to hell in a handbasket.

In London, a group of reformers called Puritans pushed to clean up society and "purify" the Anglican Church. Anything that smacked too much of Roman Catholicism, such as ornate crosses, incense, and colorful ministers' robes, raised the Puritans' ire. Anne's family agreed with the Puritans, but the risk of more jail time kept their lips zipped tight for a while. Besides, Anne was young and eager to start her own family. She left the agitating to others and married Will, the boy next door from back in Alford.

For 20 years, Will Hutchinson ran a business selling fabric, while Anne followed in her fertile mother's footsteps and had a dozen children. She also attended births and advised women about spiritual concerns. Many ministers would not have approved of this lay ministry, but Anne's Puritan-leaning minister, Reverend John Cotton, said, "You are doing God's work, Mistress Hutchinson!"

The roly-poly Reverend Cotton did not look like much, but he was Anne's guru. When Cotton risked his Anglican superiors' wrath by taking down the ornate altar cross and ditching his colorful robes for basic black, Anne felt a deep spiritual awakening. One day, while praying fervently, she heard God tell her that two of her young daughters would soon die and ascend into heaven.

In those days, claiming to talk directly to God was dangerous (it smacked of witchcraft). God talked to ministers once in a blue moon, but not to ordinary people. Anne knew this, yet when the prophecy came true and her daughters grew ill and died, she confessed all to Reverend Cotton. The minister wrinkled his brow and warned. "This is highly unusual Mistress Hutchinson. If I didn't know of your goodness, I would think ye an agent of the Devil. You'd best keep this under your bonnet."

Anne did keep her vision secret, which was wise because vocal Puritans were landing in the clinker right and left. In 1630, Reverend Cotton had finally had enough of Anglican restrictions and led a few hundred Puritan reformers to the New World. Four years later, Anne and her family followed him. "Massachusetts is a Garden of Eden for true believers," Anne told her children. " God will protect us from pirates and savages."

What Anne didn't know was that she'd need protection from her own kind! Although she planned to be good, something loosened her tongue. While sailing to Massachusetts, she debated religious dogma with the onboard minister—and boasted about her chats with the Lord. As soon as the ship docked, that horrified reverend rushed to see the church leaders in Boston. "Question this woman carefully before you let her join the church," he warned. "She is full of sinful pride!"

Before Anne could get herself in more trouble, Reverend Cotton pulled her aside and whispered urgently, "You're not in England anymore, Mistress Hutchinson. There we banded together to protect each other. Here you must be tactful and hold your tongue!" Exhausted from the journey across the Atlantic, Anne caved in. When the church elders summoned her to answer the charge of uttering blasphemy, Anne cast her eyes to the floor. "I had wrong thoughts," she confessed meekly. "Please forgive me." Tickled by this humble attitude, the church admitted Anne as a full member of the church.

In Boston, Anne and her family built a fine stone house near Governor John Winthrop and settled down quietly in the village of cod fishers, shipbuilders, cobblers, and blacksmiths. William Hutchinson quickly reestablished his bustling business selling cloth.

It didn't take long for Anne to learn that Puritans were bent on creating a completely sin-free society. To make sure that happened, they ruled Massachusetts with an iron fist. The General Court, which Winthrop headed, enforced scads of laws controlling everyone's daily lives. If you fell asleep, whispered, or smiled in church, watch out! A watchman might rap you lightly on the head with a long stick or tickle your nose with a feather. If a wife talked back to her husband, she might be dunked in a river or pond, tied to a dunking stool. If you stole a silver spoon, you were put in the stocks, and people threw apples and dirt at you. If you stole another, you could be hanged!

Of course, all the laws in the world couldn't make people into saints, and superstrict rules inspired rebellion. During Anne's first years in Boston, small groups of heretics (those who spoke against the church) left Massachusetts or were kicked out. The renegades founded Rhode Island, New Hampshire, and Connecticut. All of these rebels were men—until Anne got in on the act!

★ ★ ★ ★ ★ ★ ★ ★ ★ ★ ★ ★ ★ ★ ★ ★ ★ ★

As the first woman to make waves, Anne really got the Puritans' knickers in a twist. Her troubles started when she began holding prayer meetings for the women of Boston. At first, Anne tamely repeated the ministers' sermons, but after a while, her own ideas burst free. When the Puritan leaders heard those ideas, their discomfort with Anne's independence turned to outrage! The Puritan leaders said that only an elect few could get to heaven (including themselves, of course). In contrast, Anne preached that all of the faithful would find salvation. The Puritans preached that Jesus said men were the masters of women; Anne preached that Jesus said men and women were equal.

Winthrop sputtered that Anne's unorthodox views were diabolical, and she was stepping out of her ordained place: "Women are the weaker vessel and must be silent. She must be guided by her husband and her minister!" Although powerful friends protected Anne at first, the General Court soon passed a law forbidding women to preach to more than 60 people. Anne disobeyed and was arrested.

Middle-aged and pregnant with her last child, Anne Hutchinson defended herself before the court in 1637. In spite of themselves, the 50 ministers and magistrates who heard her case were

ANNE'S COURTROOM DEFENSE EVEN WOWED THE JUDGES WHO BANISHED HER.

★ ★ ★ ★ ★ ★ ★ ★ ★ ★ ★ ★ ★ ★ ★ ★ ★ ★

wowed by her knowledge of biblical passages. They were about to let her off with a warning when a wave of glorious victory surged through Anne. Impulsively, she blurted at the court, "I knew God would save me from you!"

At that, the offended judges did an about-face. Governor Winthrop bellowed that Anne was an American Jezebel. (In the Old Testament, Jezebel killed God's prophets and was eaten by the dogs for her wickedness.) "Mistress Hutchinson, you have been a husband rather than a wife! A preacher rather than a hearer! A magistrate rather than a subject! We offer you up to Satan and banish you from Massachusetts forever!" Winthrop pronounced.

★ ★ ★ ★ ★ ★ ★ ★ ★ ★ ★ ★ ★ ★ ★ ★ ★ ★

A QUAKER MARTYR

When Anne Hutchinson was banished, her good friend Mary Dyer walked out of the court proceedings in protest. For that, she and her husband William were also banished from Massachusetts and settled near the Hutchinsons in Newport, Rhode Island. By 1657, Mary had converted to Quakerism, a faith that shared many of Anne Hutchinson's beliefs. In 1657, Mary decided to protest the "wicked and bloody" law that banned Quakers from Massachusetts—under punishment of death. The first two times Mary trespassed in Massachusetts, she was released. The third time, on June 1, 1660, she was hanged.

Quakers inspired by the courage of Mary's convictions continued to break the anti-Quaker laws. More people protested against the persecution of Quakers, and the King of England bowed to pressure and banned death sentences against Quakers in the colonies.

★ ★ ★ ★ ★ ★ ★ ★ ★ ★ ★ ★ ★ ★ ★ ★ ★ ★

In 1638, Anne and her family left Massachusetts for the boondocks of Rhode Island. Anne lived in exile with other dissidents for four years and was friendly with the nearby Narragansett tribe. By the early 1640s, however, a worried Anne felt very unsafe. Her husband had died, and Massachusetts was scheming to take over surrounding colonies. Anne felt she'd be safer in Dutch-held Long Island and moved there with her children.

In fact, however, Anne wasn't safer at all. The Dutch director-general at the time, William Kieft, hated Native Americans and had found many excuses to make their lives miserable. In 1643, a group of tribes in the lower Hudson Valley—the Tappan, Hackensack, Raritan, Kitchawank, Manhattan, Massapequa, and others—took revenge on the Dutch colonists. They attacked settlers in outlying areas of the colony. In one bloody attack, Anne Hutchinson and five of her children were killed.

When people who never dreamed of breaking church law learned of Anne's death, they felt that colonial leaders had gone too far. A devout woman had been forced into exile—and her family slaughtered—all because she had spoken her own mind in a prayer session! More malcontents left Massachusetts for Rhode Island, New Hampshire, Connecticut, and other New England colonies. Anne Hutchinson's death spurred the movement toward religious liberty on American soil.

CHAPTER 2

★ ★ ★ ★ ★ ★ ★ ★ ★ ★

Queen Weetamoo

(1 6 3 ? – 1 6 6 7)

You probably know that in 1620, a bunch of starving Pilgrims tumbled out of the *Mayflower* at a place they dubbed Plymouth Rock. Then friendly Native Americans rescued them, and everyone shared a gigantic feast we call the first Thanksgiving. The chances are good, however, that you've never heard about the true heroine of the Wampanoag, the tribe that helped the Pilgrims. Her name was Queen Weetamoo, and when it came her turn to rule as chief, she shut down the welcome wagon! Weetamoo turned against the land-hungry Pilgrims and Puritans and fought courageously to protect her people.

When the first Pilgrims landed, Corbitant, Weetamoo's father, was the chief of a Wampanoag village called Pocasset (in present-day Rhode Island). The religious Pilgrims thought the Wampanoag were naked savages and heathens but desperately needed their help to survive in the hostile wilderness. The Wampanoag, which means "people of the first light," thought the white newcomers were pretty ugly—all that pale skin and those hairy chins. But on the other hand, the pale-faced strangers had grand sailing ships and interesting new trade goods, so the Pilgrims and the Wampanoag negotiated trade, land, and military alliances. Both peoples thought, "Hmmm, this alliance should be good for everyone."

Weetamoo was born in the early 1630s, about a decade after the Pilgrims had landed. By that time, the village of Plymouth was well established, but the Puritan invasion hadn't yet transformed her tribe's way of life. Weetamoo grew up living as her people had for generations. In the rocky soil they grew corn and squash, and on the beaches of coastal sea islands they collected shells used for everything from utensils to jewelry. From canoes made of logs and

★ ★ ★ ★ ★ ★ ★ ★ ★ ★ ★ ★ ★ ★ ★ ★ ★ ★

THE FIRST THANKSGIVING

The Wampanoag and the Pilgrims did gather at a harvest feast and thanked their different gods before breaking bread, but Thanksgiving did not become an official holiday until 1863.

Unlike today, stuffed turkey, baked ham, cranberry sauce, yams, and pumpkin pie weren't on the menu at the first harvest feast. Instead, everyone dined on deer, fish, clams, oysters, lobster, ducks, swans, and Indian corn. To drink, there was brandy, gin, wine, and, especially, beer. Pure drinking water had been hard to come by in Europe, so everyone—men, women, and children—drank ale, beer, and rum with their meals. In fact, the Puritans loaded more beer than water onto the *Mayflower*!

Understandably, many native people consider Thanksgiving a day of mourning, not celebration. After all, the New England natives vastly outnumbered the first white settlers. If they'd sent the strange white folks packing, who knows what America would look like today.

★ ★ ★ ★ ★ ★ ★ ★ ★ ★ ★ ★ ★ ★ ★ ★ ★ ★

bark, they caught cod and other fish. In the frigid winters, Weetamoo's people left the shore and went deep into New England's forests. The forest provided abundant game, wood for fires, and saplings for building round huts called wetus. Their simple way of living left plenty of time for singing, dancing, feasting, playing lively ball games, and celebrating festivals where large extended families, called clans, came together.

Weetamoo's childhood was happy because of these joys, yet as Weetamoo grew, troubles beset the tribe. The Europeans brought new diseases, and many natives died. By the time Weetamoo was 10 years old, the Wampanoag had gone from a population of 10,000 to half that. Meanwhile the white population of New England doubled.

Every morning, Weetamoo left her family's wetu and greeted the first rosy light of dawn. With the other village women and girls, she planted corn, fixed meals, sewed clothing, tanned hides, gathered herbs, and managed the village. Weetamoo's mother's name is lost, but as a chief's wife, she probably sat on a council of women that made decisions about marriages, child rearing, home ownership, and farming. Meanwhile, a council of men made decisions about war, hunting, trade, and territory.

By the time Weetamoo was a teenager, Wampanoag society had been changed forever by white contact. To get furs, which were very much in demand by the Europeans, Wampanoag men traveled farther inland to hunt. They were often gone for several months. When the hunters came home, the women had to leave the fields and start tanning hides. With less time to farm, the Wampanoag didn't just want the cool stuff whites offered—they needed it. Wheat flour and calico replaced cornmeal and deerskin robes. Iron tools and weapons replaced those made of wood and stone.

Weetamoo also met her share of Puritan missionaries, who came visiting with Bibles tucked under their arms. When one prayed for the end of a six-week drought and down came the rain, the people were impressed. Then Chief Massasoit grew ill and the missionary cured him with white men's medicine (including chicken soup). After that, the chief became a Christian. He renamed his sons Metacomet and Wamsutta, Philip and Alexander.

In the 1650s, Weetamoo married Alexander, who became head chief when his father died in 1660. In a soft doeskin dress embroidered with white shell beads and goose feathers, Weetamoo stood before the gathered people. The white decorations symbolized peace and harmony. Alexander, draped in a black wolf skin and beads made from antlers and shells, stood by Weetamoo's side. As the couple promised to keep each other safe and warm, the future seemed bright.

Despite this promising future, Head Chief Alexander assumed leadership at a dangerous time for the Wampanoag. The "Merry Monarch," Charles II, took the throne in England. Thanks to the king's wanton ways—including scads of mistresses and illegitimate children—the Puritans *really* didn't like him. Thousands more Puritans fled to the New World and settled on Wampanoag and other native-owned land.

To make matters even worse, the bottom dropped out of the fur market in Europe. Suddenly the Wampanoag were no longer coveted trading partners, and the Puritans' bigotry showed itself: "We forbid you to sell any land without our approval," Massachusetts leaders haughtily ordered the Wampanoag.

Chief Alexander was a much tougher bird than his father had been, though, and wasn't as willing to bend to the Puritans' commands. Under his leadership, the tribe refused to heed the bossy whites' pronouncements and sold land when it pleased. For this defiance, Weetamoo's husband paid with his life.

The Massachusetts officials invited Alexander for "talks" then seized him at gunpoint! In captivity, he ate the white men's food, became violently ill, and died. Weetamoo was told he died of a fever but was convinced he'd been poisoned. Weetamoo may have been right about that, for records show that the Plymouth Council bought a batch of poison right about that time. "We must rid ourselves of a pest," the record reads.

When Alexander died, his brother Philip took over as head chief. Whites called him King Philip. Weetamoo became a chief of Pocasset about the same time, when her father Corbitant died. Whites called her Queen Weetamoo, a name that soon struck terror in the hearts of southern New England whites. Whites thought

★ ★ ★ ★ ★ ★ ★ ★ ★ ★ ★ ★ ★ ★ ★ ★ ★ ★

HAIL TO THE CHIEFTESS!

Native American women had a lot more power and status than colonial white women did. Many tribes were *matrilineal*—children took their mothers' names, not their fathers'. In such tribes, separate women's and men's councils governed different aspects of village life. Men saw to hunting and war. Women ruled the village and farms.

Women chiefs—also called queens—were rare, but women did reign now and then. Among the Cherokee women, leaders called Beloved or Honored Women could veto decisions to go to war. In other nations, women like Weetamoo inherited leadership positions when there were no male heirs— or got the jobs because the people agreed they had the right stuff to lead.

★ ★ ★ ★ ★ ★ ★ ★ ★ ★ ★ ★ ★ ★ ★ ★ ★ ★

Weetamoo was grand looking, but insolent as all get out. "Queen Weetamoo spends as much time as the gentry dressing!" a white woman who visited her remarked. "She preens about in a mix of fine brocade, animal hides, and jeweled necklaces. She even powders her hair like a Duchess at the Royal Court!"

Actually, Weetamoo wore her finery—and her new mantle of power—very well. Both she and King Philip were determined to hold onto the land left to their people. "My people were like loving parents to you when you first arrived on our land," she scolded the colonists. "Now you have a hundred times more land than our people, yet you want more. While I am queen, you shall not have it."

Weetamoo stood firm even though she was up against a powerful foe, which grew even stronger after England captured New York from the Dutch in 1664. Weetamoo told the 300 warriors under her command, "We will have no land left if we don't take a stand!" At a great tribal gathering, most Wampanoag leaders agreed with Weetamoo. A handful, however, voted to give the English what they wanted, including Petonowowett, Weetamoo's second husband. He stood before the chiefs and declared, "I am a loyal subject of the king!" I bet you can guess what happened after that: Weetamoo tossed her husband's bedroll and tomahawk out the door of their wetu! "You are no longer my husband," Weetamoo announced, and they were divorced.

In 1665, the Wampanoag chiefs drew a line in the sand and warned the whites, "If any of you trespass on this land, we will wage war." When the whites ignored the threat, a thousand warriors under the command of Philip and Weetamoo crept up on villages and homes all over southern New England. From wilderness hideouts, they launched King Philip's War. The New Englanders never knew what hit them, for the Wampanoag were skilled in ambush. They gunned down people strolling to Sunday meeting, picked off sentries outside forts, burned down 20 towns, and took dozens of captives.

The outnumbered Wampanoag didn't keep their advantage for long, however, for the colonists abandoned traditional European warfare and did their own ambushing. Wampanoag villages and fields were burned, and 400 women and children of the neutral Narragansett tribe were massacred. Weetamoo was fit to be tied about the massacre, and so were the Narragansett, who joined the war. All over New England, colonists said to their children, "Don't venture out of the yard, or Queen Weetamoo will get you!"

The warnings were wise, for during the war, the Native American army took dozens of white captives. Torture, death, enslavement, or adoption into the tribe (to replace dead family members) was the captives' fates. Some were also exchanged for imprisoned tribe members or held for ransom. Mary Rowlandson, an upright minister's wife from Lancaster, Massachusetts, later wrote about her experiences as Weetamoo's captive slave. When Mary grew tired from staggering through frigid creeks while on the run, Weetamoo mocked her. When the captive refused to stop reading her Bible and get to work cooking or cleaning, Weetamoo slapped her face. "The hell-hound acted above herself in class and race!" Mary Rowlandson huffed after she was ransomed.

Despite their many victories, the Wampanoag and Narragansett tribes were outnumbered. Winter arrived and they retreated to the Berkshire hills of New York. Their crops had been burned to ashes, and game was scarce. Dried roots and berries barely kept the people alive through the bitter cold months. When spring finally arrived, the bone-thin warriors could not defeat the well-fed colonial reinforcements. The warriors had destroyed 20 colonial towns and killed 600 whites, but the whites' conquest of them was at hand. Weetamoo's third husband, Quanopin, was captured and shot by a firing squad. Her sister was sold into slavery. She herself fled with two dozen others to an area of Rhode Island called Gardiner's Neck.

The pursuing army caught up with Weetamoo's group and killed everyone—except wily Weetamoo herself. Somehow she escaped the soldiers, built a rickety raft, and tried to ford a swollen river. Unfortunately, in the raging rapids, the raft shattered, and brave Weetamoo met her end. The soldiers, still in pursuit, found her drowned body washed up on the shore. They cut off her head, wrapped it in a blanket, and impaled it on a pole in Taunton, Massachusetts. When Wampanoag prisoners in the

KING PHILIP MADE NEW ENGLAND OFFICIALS PAY DEARLY FOR THEIR HIGH-HANDEDNESS.

★ ★ ★ ★ ★ ★ ★ ★ ★ ★ ★ ★ ★ ★ ★ ★ ★ ★

THE REAL POCAHONTAS

Do you wonder why little-known Weetamoo is featured in this book, but not the famous Pocahontas? After all, the native princess of Virginia saved the life of Virginia Colony's John Smith, who was about to be clubbed to death by her father Chief Powhatan back in 1607—right? Wrong! You can still enjoy the Disney movie about Pocahontas, but recognize it for what it is—a bunch of hoo-ha. In truth, John Smith was kidnapped because Powhatan's people were at war with the whites of Jamestown. Despite the war, Smith wrote in his journal that Chief Powhatan treated him kindly. Smith didn't mention Pocahontas at all, let alone her saving his life. In fact, it wasn't until years later that Smith told the rescue story (along with other trumped-up tales).

The real Pocahontas was, sadly, a victim of politics and greed. When she was 17, Jamestown whites took her prisoner and held her for a year. Her captors aimed to force her father to give up more land. During her captivity, a 28-year-old widower named John Rolfe married Pocahontas, now called Rebecca. Maybe it was for love. Maybe it was to encourage Powhatan to treat the whites as favored relatives. Maybe it was both, but no one really knows for sure.

Two years later, Rolfe took "Rebecca" to England. There, the Virginia Company of London used her in its propaganda campaign to support the colony. The damp, foggy London weather made Pocahontas gravely ill, and she died in England at age 21. Only *after* her death did John Smith began spinning his famous yarn that made Chief Powhatan look like a brutal beast. That helped the English justify what happened next. Powhatan and his people were slaughtered and robbed of their land. Across the New World, other tribes met the same fate.

nearby jail saw their queen's head displayed, they wailed for days. Before the end of the week, King Philip's head was on display, too.

After King Philip's War, the Native American death toll was in the thousands. Weetamoo and her people were nearly extinguished, but several hundred escaped into the forest. Some joined other tribes; others held fast to their roots and many years later sued successfully to get back some of their land. Today, 4,000 descendants of the Wampanoag and related tribes live in southern New England. Several hundred Wampanoag own ancestral land on Martha's Vineyard, off the coast of Cape Cod. Against all odds, Weetamoo's people endured the European invasion of their homelands—and survived.

★ ★ ★ ★ ★ ★ ★ ★ ★ ★

CHAPTER 3

Deborah Samson

(1760 - 1831)

In 1775, 15-year-old Deborah Samson watched the boys and men of Middleboro, Massachusetts, march down the dirt road to fight the British in Concord. "I can run as fast as any of them. I can shoot just as straight. I wish I could join them!" Deborah thought. Instead, she had to cook, sew, spin, and do farm work. However, convention couldn't hold Deborah Samson (sometimes spelled Sampson) forever. She never stopped dreaming of being a soldier, and a few years later she made her dream a reality.

Deborah was born into a respectable New England clan on December 17, 1760. Some of her ancestors, including John and Priscilla Alden, had sailed to America on the *Mayflower*. Despite her family's venerable background, Deborah's father was a mess. He drank too much and let their farm go to ruin. By the time Deborah was five years old, he had abandoned his wife and five children for good. The motto on the family's coat of arms read, "Disgrace is worse than death." Deborah was deeply ashamed that her own father hadn't lived up to that lofty family motto!

★ ★ ★ ★ ★ ★ ★ ★ ★ ★ ★ ★ ★ ★ ★ ★ ★ ★ ★

AMERICAN-BORN SERVANTS

In the American colonies, struggling families like Deborah Samson's often "bound out" their children as indentured servants. For room and board, children were bound out to work for their masters until they were 18. Most female servants married as soon as they were free, for there was no shortage of men waiting to snatch them up. For every single woman, there were several single men!

★ ★ ★ ★ ★ ★ ★ ★ ★ ★ ★ ★ ★ ★ ★ ★ ★ ★

After her father's disappearance, Deborah's mother went to live with a relative and "bound out" Deborah and her brothers as indentured servants. Being an indentured servant was like being a temporary slave. Because the servitude was temporary—usually just a few years—the master didn't have life-or-death control over the servant's body. Also, in exchange for her labor, Deborah got a roof over her head and food in her belly.

Luckily, she ended up with the kind and rambunctious Thomas family, which had 10 rowdy sons! On a big, bustling farm, Deborah helped her mistress in the house. Then she dashed off to do what she *really* loved—working side-by-side with the boys. Deborah tended livestock, made hay, and shot game with a musket. Outside work made hardy Deborah feel as happy as a colt in springtime.

At age 18, Deborah completed her years of indentured service. Her mother expected her to marry right away, as other freed indentured servant girls did. Deborah had a long horsy face, and many people thought she was plain. That didn't matter, though, because Deborah was hardworking, responsible, a skilled house-

★ ★ ★ ★ ★ ★ ★ ★ ★ ★ ★ ★ ★ ★ ★ ★ ★ ★

keeper—a good catch! A successful merchant proposed right away, but Deborah surprised everyone by refusing him. "He's a baboon and too fond of whetting his whistle with rum," she fumed.

The shocked Thomases poured on the pressure, but Deborah stuck to her guns. Determined to be independent, she hired herself out as a traveling weaver. Normally, only poor widows without relatives to take them in worked at such jobs. With no home of her own, Deborah moved from house to house doing people's spinning and weaving. Her bed was a corn-shuck mattress in a corner; the pay was a pittance. Although this life was better than marrying a lout she didn't love, Deborah was also bored stiff. Outside, the battle for independence raged, and Deborah wracked her brain for a way out of her life of drudgery.

At age 22, Deborah couldn't stand it a minute longer. Late at night, she secretly plied her needle. Then she bound her chest with linen cloth, tied her long brown hair into a ponytail and

★ ★ ★ ★ ★ ★ ★ ★ ★ ★ ★ ★ ★ ★ ★ ★ ★ ★

AMERICA'S FIRST HEALERS

Deborah Samson wasn't the only female at West Point. Many camp followers, including paid nurses, were also stationed there. Civilians such as Martha Ballard of rural Maine worked as community health workers, too. She prescribed medicine, prepared burials, did autopsies—and delivered more than 800 babies! Another woman, Kernhappuck Turner of Maryland, rode all the way to North Carolina to nurse her wounded grandson back to health after a battle. The clever grandma bored holes in a large tub of cool water and mounted it on rafters above him. The water dripped from holes into his wound to keep it clean!

★ ★ ★ ★ ★ ★ ★ ★ ★ ★ ★ ★ ★ ★ ★ ★ ★ ★

donned her new manly suit of brown homespun. After slipping out the door of her employer, she hurried down the road to the Continental Army recruiting office in Worcester. On May 20, 1782, Deborah enlisted, using the name Robert Shurtliff. With that act, she made history as the first female soldier in America.

The army was more than glad to have another able body, even though the war was winding down. Seven months earlier, the British General Cornwallis had surrendered in Yorktown, Virginia. Final peace negotiations would take two more years, however, and many Loyalists (colonists loyal to Britain) refused to admit defeat. With other new recruits, Deborah marched toward New York. Trumpets blared, the fife trilled, and soldiers sang Yankee songs to British marching tunes. Deborah marched through pouring rain and slept in her clothes—and wondered if she'd made a huge mistake! Although tough, she wasn't used to *this* kind of hard living. Exhausted, she staggered against the other men, then looked around to see whether anyone suspected her secret. She realized, however, that other recruits were staggering, too. The fatigue was so great that Deborah fainted once—and awoke to find a tavern maid murmuring sweet nothings in her ear! Deborah thought, "She thinks I'm a man!" and bolted out of the girl's arms.

The recruits finally arrived at West Point, which perched on gigantic cliffs above New York's deep Hudson River. The light infantry of the 4th Massachusetts Regiment of the Army issued Deborah a dashing blue and white uniform with bone buttons. On her head sat a hard leather helmet crested with a strip of bear fur and a fine red and black feather. Like the other soldiers, she powdered her hair with flour. Before long, she could load and fire a musket two times in a minute.

It must have been nerve-wracking, keeping her secret from 10,000 soldiers. Sharing her straw mattress with another soldier made Deborah especially nervous at first. It turned out she had nothing to worry about, though: Everyone slept in clothes, and Deborah's bedmate was out like a light when his head hit the mattress. Deborah relaxed, and no one guessed that the handsome, beardless boy named Robert was really a woman.

West Point officers soon saw that Deborah was a good shot and assigned her to a special unit of rangers. Their job was to hunt down bands of diehard Loyalists who roamed the countryside burning Patriots' homes and crops. On Deborah's first assignment, Loyalists ambushed her unit. Musket balls whizzed over her head. Smoke filled the air. The sergeant yelled, "Fire!" and Deborah fired. The man next to Deborah was struck in the chest and fell. Blood spurted on her pants. When her sergeant yelled, "Retreat!" Deborah ran faster than a jackrabbit.

The next time Deborah's unit was attacked, she wasn't so lucky. In hand-to-hand combat with a Loyalist raider, she held her ground. When she had the chance, she stabbed him with her bayonet, but then he slashed her forehead with his saber and shot her in the thigh. At a French hospital, a doctor dressed her head wound, then scurried away to tend more critically wounded patients.

According to an dramatic recounting of Deborah's life written in 1797 (*The Female Review: Memoirs of an American Young Lady* by journalist Herman Mann), she was afraid the doctor would return, discover the thigh wound, and tell her to take off her breeches. As soon as the doctor left, therefore, Deborah grabbed a curved silver probe off a tray, thrust it into the bleeding hole and twisted out the inch-deep musket ball—all without screaming!

Deborah recovered from her wounds and that winter was sent to upstate New York to round up Mohawks who had been allied with the British during the war. Like the Loyalists, the Mohawks were refusing to admit defeat. They roamed the frontier attacking remote cabins and forts, scalping men, women, and children alike. Deborah camped in the frigid wilderness and this wilderness camping left her uniform in tatters. Just when Deborah thought she couldn't take another day, her unit was sent to a winter encampment at Windsor, New York.

To Deborah, the winter camp seemed positively luxurious after weeks in the frozen wilderness. Deborah's companions grumbled a lot, however, especially about back pay owed them by the Continental Congress (now governing America). The muttering grew so intense that Congress feared a mutiny. In the spring of 1783, Deborah and a battalion of soldiers were sent to Philadelphia to guard Congress—just in case! The threats eventually died down, and across the country, diehard Loyalists and Native Americans were defeated at last. There wasn't much left for American soldiers to do, and Deborah might have whiled away her remaining years playing poker in an army tent—but she had another fate in store.

A nasty fever spread through the camp, and Deborah caught it, ending up in the Pennsylvania Hospital. There, according to Mann's book, she awoke to find a man standing over her saying, "I'll take this one's breeches before we send him to Potter's Field." Deborah may have been feverish, but she knew Potter's Field was a cemetery, and the men were undertakers! Grabbing a passing nurse's arm, she croaked, "Don't let them bury me." The nurse realized what was happening and swatted at the undertakers, "Get out of here you vultures!" she cried. "Can't you even wait till they die?!"

Deborah didn't die, though. Instead, her secret was revealed! A doctor named Binney examined her and learned the truth. He moved Deborah to his home and nursed her back to health. Although full of admiration for his charge, Dr. Binney told the truth to the flabbergasted commander of West Point.

The commander sent for Deborah and handed her an honorable discharge. He also asked Deborah to put on his daughter's dress and parade around the camp with him. Deborah did as he asked and was stunned by her former mates' reactions. A handful of soldiers who'd known Robert Shurtliff backed away as if Deborah had some kind of terrible disease. Most laughed, though, and congratulated her for pulling off such a daring escapade. "It's not possible!" they cried. "How did you trick us?"

DEBORAH
PREFERRED
RISKING HER LIFE
AS A SOLDIER TO
MARRYING A
"BABOON."

★ ★ ★ ★ ★ ★ ★ ★ ★ ★ ★ ★ ★ ★ ★ ★ ★ ★

Even before she arrived home, news of Deborah's exploits had spread throughout New England. Although her Baptist church kicked her out for being "loose and disorderly," most people found it hard to disapprove of a woman who'd been wounded in the service of their country. One of Deborah's admirers, a poor farmer named Benjamin Gannett, courted her. In 1785, she married him, and together they raised four children.

In 1797, Herman Mann's book about Deborah's exploits caught the public's fancy. The book was a hit, but Deborah made little money on the deal and needed cash for her strapped family. To profit from her fame, Deborah began touring all over the eastern seaboard, giving presentations about her wartime adventures. At the end of each performance, she thrilled audiences by putting on her uniform jacket, marching to the beat of a fife and drum, and firing her musket into the air. As clouds of smoke billowed around Deborah on stage, the audience erupted into applause and cheers!

Deborah's performances didn't make her rich, but they helped feed and educate her children. Then, when they grew up, her children helped her end her days in comfort. Four years after her death, her husband petitioned Congress for benefits due to the spouses of veterans wounded in the war. It took six years, but the government finally awarded its first ever "widower's pension." Congress wrote, "Benjamin Gannett, you are much honored to have been the husband of such a wife, and have proved yourself worthy of her."

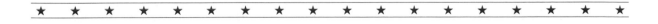

★ ★ ★ ★ ★ ★ ★ ★ ★ ★ ★

CHAPTER 4

Elizabeth "Mumbet" Freeman

(1742 – 1829)

Until she was a grown woman, Mumbet was an obedient slave. Then her mistress attacked her younger sister with a shovel, and Mumbet rebelled. When the cast-iron shovel came crashing toward her sister, Mumbet swelled with rage. As she threw her firmly packed frame between the two women, the heavy iron shovel slammed down on Mumbet's strong, brown arm.

Mumbet's sister, who was probably in her twenties, was safe. Her mistress's anger was spent—but Mumbet was still steamed. Clutching her throbbing arm, she stormed out of the only home she'd ever known—and never returned. She ditched the slave name her master had given her and took the name Elizabeth Freeman.

Born in 1742, Mumbet was the Ashley family's slave from the time she was six months old. The prominent Ashleys owned the finest house in Sheffield, a pretty village in the lush Housatonic River valley in western Massachusetts. The Berkshire hills had been good to John Ashley, who ran a general store and iron-ore

★ ★ ★ ★ ★ ★ ★ ★ ★ ★ ★ ★ ★ ★ ★ ★ ★ ★

mill. In fact, Ashley was such a local bigwig that Sheffield was later renamed Ashley Falls.

Early in life, Mumbet learned that her lot was to eat pot pies made from deer scraps, while her owners dined on plump, juicy cuts of meat. The law said she must serve, obey, and endure, and the punishment for running away was harsh.

Mumbet's life as a house slave may have been easy compared to plantation slaves in the South, but she hustled from sunup to sundown. Mumbet kept the household running like clockwork. Each day, she saw that the meals were cooked, the floors were scrubbed, and the beds were made. She washed clothes, toted water, and emptied chamber pots. While Mumbet worked she nurtured a secret. Hidden deep inside was a curious mind, an angry heart, and a soul that longed to be free!

While Mumbet was growing up, she often heard things through the slave grapevine. Every once in a while, she would learn of a few courageous whites and blacks who condemned and challenged slavery. The fiery Massachusetts lawyer James Otis said in his speeches that the slave trade violated nature's laws. A man named Samuel Sewall wrote that blacks and whites had equal rights to liberty. A few free slaves even petitioned the court to outlaw slavery.

WHILE MUMBET CLEANED AND COOKED, SHE SOAKED UP IDEAS ABOUT LIBERTY AND EQUALITY.

In 1773, Mumbet's own master also began singing the praises of freedom—for colonists. Colonel Ashley chaired a committee that wrote the anti-British Sheffield Declaration, which read much like the Declaration of Independence signed three years later. Every day, Mumbet trudged up the Ashleys' curved wooden stairway, carrying refreshments to the committee. Mumbet rested her heavy trays of rum, tea, roasted hens, and brown bread on the hand-carved cupboard. She served the men—and lingered. The committeemen had no clue that this "simple" slave woman was being influenced by their fresh, contagious ideas.

The years that followed the Sheffield Declaration were exciting, and Mumbet eagerly followed the news of the revolution. The Massachusetts militias fought British Redcoats at Concord and Lexington in 1775. The Continental Congress labored to write a Declaration of Independence, and Massachusetts worked on its Constitution and Bill of Rights. Everyone debated what should be written in the important documents. A few lone voices pushed for slavery to be outlawed. One early version of Thomas Jefferson's Declaration of Independence read, "The King has waged cruel war on human nature itself, violating its most sacred rights of life and liberty in the persons of a distant people who never offended him, captivating and carrying them into slavery in another hemisphere. . . ." How disappointed Mumbet must have been when those words were struck from the final Declaration of Independence!

Mumbet wasn't the type to wallow in disappointment, though—or to tolerate abuse. In 1781, after storming out of the Ashleys' kitchen, she headed straight to the legal office of slavery opponent Theodore Sedgewick. Mumbet told Sedgewick she wanted to sue for her freedom based on the principle that slavery was unconstitutional in Massachusetts.

Sedgewick saw in Mumbet's case a chance to challenge the new state constitution, which legalized slavery in Massachusetts. Other Berkshire County abolitionists adopted Mumbet's cause with gusto. In taverns and in newspapers they cried, "We want to be free of slavery from Britain, so we cannot tolerate slavery of others in America!" Another Ashley family slave named Brom also joined the lawsuit. In 1781, before the Court of Common Pleas in Great Barrington, Ashley argued that the Negroes he "owned" were his legal servants for life. To Ashley's horror, however, the jury of white men ruled that the general principles of freedom stated in the state constitution overruled his arguments. Not only that, Ashley had to pay Mumbet and Brom back wages—plus court costs!

As a free woman, Mumbet dumped the name her master and mistress had given her and became Elizabeth Freeman. When word spread through New England that slaves were freed by a court of law, the floodgates opened. A slough of slaves began petitioning courts for their freedom. In 1783, the Massachusetts legislature realized the writing was on the wall. Thanks in part to Mumbet's determination, slavery was abolished in the state of Massachusetts.

Through the trial, the Sedgewick family and Elizabeth had grown close. Theodore Sedgewick—congressional delegate, speaker

AFTER WINNING HER FREEDOM IN THE COURTS, MUMBET CHANGED HER NAME TO ELIZABETH FREEMAN.

★ ★ ★ ★ ★ ★ ★ ★ ★ ★ ★ ★ ★ ★ ★ ★ ★ ★

"MAMMY" KATE

Most stories of colonial African Americans are lost, but the Heard family of Georgia tells a remarkable story about the heroism of a southern slave woman called "Mammy" Kate. In 1779, at Kettle Creek in Georgia, Loyalists captured Governor Stephen Heard and threw him in prison at Fort Cornwallis. Heard's slave Kate (said to be descended from African royalty) heard the news. Kate hopped on an Arabian horse named Lightfoot, galloped to the fort, and hid Lightfoot nearby. Then she placed a big basket on her head, waltzed to the gate, and offered to do washing for the British officers. Not one to turn down expert laundering of their ruffled shirts, the officers hired her. After a while, she asked to do Governor Heard's washing. "He won't need them, for we'll soon hang that rebel," the jailer said. "I need work; let him hang in clean clothes," suggested Kate.

Twice a week, Kate visited Heard and did his laundry. Then one evening she walked out the gate with her basket on her head. It was a very heavy load she carried that day, but thankfully the guard took no notice. Inside the basket was Governor Heard (a fairly short fellow!). Never again was Mammy Kate or Governor Heard seen at Fort Cornwallis. In gratitude, the governor freed Kate and gave her a four-room home of her own.

of the U.S. House, and state court judge—asked Elizabeth to watch over his dying wife. Elizabeth agreed, and when his wife died a year later, Elizabeth stayed to raise the children and run the household. When the children were grown, Elizabeth built a fine house and struck out on her own. Until her death in her eighties, she worked in Sheffield as a paid midwife and nurse.

When Elizabeth died in 1829, she was not buried with other slaves and servants. Instead, the Sedgewicks buried her in a prominent resting place in their pie-shaped family plot. On Elizabeth's tombstone, Catherine Sedgewick (Theodore's daughter) had these words engraved: "Elizabeth Freeman, known by the name of Mumbet, was born a slave and remained a slave for nearly thirty years. She could neither read nor write, yet in her own sphere she had no superior nor equal. She neither wasted time nor property. She never violated a trust, nor failed to perform a duty. In every situation of domestic trial, she was the most efficient helper, and the tenderest friend. Good Mother, farewell."

★ ★ ★ ★ ★ ★ ★ ★ ★ ★

CHAPTER 5

Abigail Smith Adams

(1744 - 1818)

A s her husband John huddled with Thomas Jefferson drafting the Declaration of Independence, Abigail Adams urged him to include rights for women: "Dearest Partner," she wrote, "American men should give up the harsh title of Master for the more tender and endearing one of friend. Remember the ladies!" This folderol about women's rights didn't sit too well with her husband, but Abigail wasn't silenced. She couldn't be, for as she wrote, "My bursting heart must find vent at my pen!"

Abigail's burning desire to write about public affairs did not surprise those who knew her well. When she was a child growing up in Weymouth, Massachusetts, her mother fretted about her daughter's "unwomanly" interest in history, literature, and politics. Abigail's feisty Grandmother Quincy said not to worry, though: "Wild colts make good horses."

As a 15-year-old wild colt, Abigail first met the 25-year-old Bay State lawyer, John Adams. This plump, clever descendant of

★ ★ ★ ★ ★ ★ ★ ★ ★ ★ ★ ★ ★ ★ ★ ★ ★ ★ ★

constables, surveyors, and shopkeepers pleased Abigail. John, in turn, liked Abigail, the keen-eyed descendant of shipbuilders, lawyers, and judges. Abigail's family had hoped for a more aristocratic suitor, but their daughter was madly in love! "I no sooner close my eyes than some invisible being bears me to you," Abigail cooed to her absent suitor. "My heart and body have been thrown into disorder by your absence," an equally loving John replied.

By 1764, Abigail's family relented. She and John married and moved to Braintree, Massachusetts. John built his country law practice, and Abigail gave birth to the first of five children. John's clients had a hard time paying their bills, though, because of new British taxes and trade laws that limited what colonists could manufacture and export. "We can't manufacture buttons, horse-shoes, or hob nails without the British bawling and squalling," John's clients complained. "We'll have to owe you, John."

ABIGAIL ADAMS' LETTERS INSPIRED GENERATIONS OF WOMEN.

In search of better prospects, Abigail and John moved to nearby Boston. The second-largest colonial city in North America bustled with trade and commerce. Bolts of cloth, stacks of lumber, and nets filled with fish littered the docks, awaiting shipment to Europe. Horse-drawn wagons pushed their way through the narrow dirt and cobblestone streets. Abigail loved shopping in the open market and strolling in the common. The future looked brighter in the big city.

★ ★ ★ ★ ★ ★ ★ ★ ★ ★ ★ ★ ★ ★ ★ ★ ★ ★

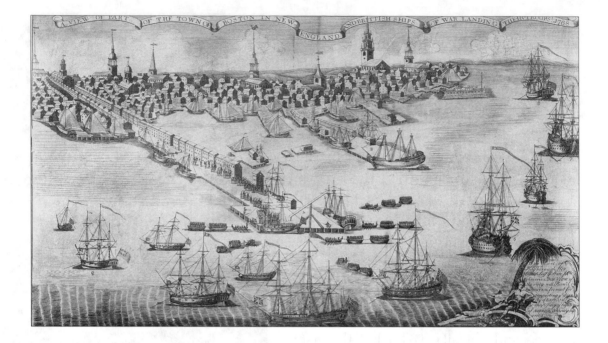

BRITISH REDCOATS CLOGGING BOSTON HARBOR HEIGHTENED COLONIAL OUTRAGE.

Yet beneath Boston's cheerful hustle and bustle, trouble lurked. Redcoats drilling daily in the cobblestone streets were an unwelcome reminder of Britain's power. Trouble soon came calling at the door of Abigail's brick house on Brattle Square. In March 1770, heavily pregnant with her third child, a worried Abigail watched hundreds of Bostonians swarm past her window like angry bees. Armed with sticks and clubs they shouted anti-British slogans. All over town, church bells tolled, as they did during fires. Abigail drew the curtains, locked the door, and put the children to bed. Then she went downstairs to wait and worry. John was at one of his secret Sons of Liberty meetings! Was he safe? Was she? Were her children?

★ ★ ★ ★ ★ ★ ★ ★ ★ ★ ★ ★ ★ ★ ★ ★

★ ★ ★ ★ ★ ★ ★ ★ ★ ★ ★ ★ ★ ★ ★ ★ ★ ★

LOVE EARLY AMERICAN STYLE

Oddly enough, considering their Puritan forefathers (and foremothers), colonial New Englanders had the most romantic notions about marriage. Love was considered an important ingredient for a happy marriage, so young people played the field before choosing a mate (and asking their parents' permission). There was even an odd courting custom called "bundling," in which a boyfriend and girlfriend spent the night together, in the same bed. A wooden board running down the middle of the bed kept the sweethearts safely separate!

★ ★ ★ ★ ★ ★ ★ ★ ★ ★ ★ ★ ★ ★ ★ ★ ★ ★

At last, John returned and Abigail let him in. A mob had cornered several British guards at the Boston Customs (tax collection) House, he said. To gather a bigger crowd, boys had rung the church bells. Soon a hysterical crowd of thousands was throwing icicles, rocks, and snowballs at the soldiers. "Fire, damn you, fire!" the crowd taunted the soldiers. "You dare not fire! Fire! Fire! Fire!" Panicked, confused, and cornered, the soldiers fired. When the smoke cleared, five American colonists lay dead in the snow.

As punishment for what was soon called the "Boston Massacre," King George III closed Boston Harbor. "The die is now cast," King George said. "The colonies must either submit or perish!" Riots and protests followed, including the Boston Tea Party in December 1773. When the protestors dumped hundreds of barrels of "baneful weed" into the harbor, Abigail strongly approved. "The flame is kindled and like Lightning it catches from Soul to Soul," she wrote to her friend, Mercy Warren.

★ ★ ★ ★ ★ ★ ★ ★ ★ ★ ★ ★ ★ ★ ★ ★ ★ ★

War seemed inevitable, and John galloped off to Philadelphia to represent Massachusetts in the Continental Congress. Meanwhile, Abigail and her household fled from the city to the farm in Braintree.

From a nearby hilltop on the farm, Abigail could see Boston. On June 17, 1775, she heard distant thuds of cannon fire and dashed to the crest of moonlit Pens Hill. In the distant valley, tiny figures of American Rebels and British Redcoats swarmed over Bunker Hill and Breeds Hill. Musket and cannon fire ripped through the silence. Flames engulfed Charles Town.

The battle raged all night, and the next day, Abigail learned the outcome. The British still occupied Boston, but their victory had been hard won. A thousand British were dead or wounded, as were 400 Americans. Abigail sat down at her writing desk, picked

★ ★ ★ ★ ★ ★ ★ ★ ★ ★ ★ ★ ★ ★ ★ ★ ★ ★

RUMBLINGS OF REBELLION

In the 1760s, the British beefed up their military presence in the American colonies. A "quartering" law ordered colonists to house and feed British officers in their homes. The British said the colonists should pay for the Redcoats' upkeep, for they were there to protect the colonists. That explanation seemed ridiculous to the colonists, though, for there was nothing they needed protection from!

Most colonists firmly believed the British soldiers were there to enforce unpopular laws and taxes and to scare the colonists into complying with British laws. Having people 3,000 miles away telling them what to do had been bad enough. Having a standing army around to crack the whip was intolerable. Fed up, the colonists proceeded to boycott, petition, and agitate. When none of that worked, they waged war against the British.

★ ★ ★ ★ ★ ★ ★ ★ ★ ★ ★ ★ ★ ★ ★ ★ ★ ★

up her quill pen and wrote again to her husband John in Philadel-phia. Abigail poured out her grief over fallen friends and offered her own brand of support! "If all the American men were to be killed, the women would take up arms and drive out the tyrants!"

Fortunately, enough men managed to stay alive, so that the women didn't have to take up arms. The men certainly couldn't have managed without women like Abigail, though. Someone had to manage the farms, raise the children, melt pewter dishes down to make bullets, and feed refugees. For Abigail, this was no piece of cake. British warships appeared offshore, terrifying everyone. A smallpox epidemic sickened the entire household. Farmhands left in the middle of haymaking season to join the Continental Army. The army took cattle, malt, and cider to feed the soldiers, and money was so tight that Abigail could not afford to repair the crumbling ceiling and moldy floor!

Coping with this mess made Abigail feel she wore a heavy millstone around her neck. In letter after letter, she begged John to return home—or at least to send more money! Unfortunately, however, her politician husband had big fish to fry but little cash to send. At last, Abigail realized she must rescue the family fi-nances without his help. She threw herself into studying farming and raised bumper crops. As a sideline, she also imported scarce goods from Europe and resold them at a tidy profit. No longer did Abigail plead and beg. Now she crowed, "I am proud to tell you, John. I have become quite the merchant and farmeress!"

After the British finally left Massachusetts in March 1776, Abigail turned her mind to politics. When John was helping to write the Declaration of Independence, she showered him with questions. "If a government is to be established here, will our colonial assemblies choose the form?" Abigail asked. "Will not many men have many minds?" She also offered her suggestions about women's rights. Under English law, married women could not own property, sign contracts, transact business, or draft wills. Abigail decided this was wrong! "Dearest partner," she wrote, "Remember the Ladies and be more generous and favorable to them than your ancestors. Do not put such unlimited power into the hands of Husbands. Remember all Men would be tyrants if they could."

Before Abigail made this suggestion, John had praised her as, "my top advisor." But he disliked this lobbying about women's rights. "As to your extraordinary Code of Laws, I cannot but laugh," a high and mighty John replied. "Depend upon it, we know better than to repeal our masculine systems!" Although miffed, Abigail merely changed the subject for awhile. "John, you must outlaw slavery and improve schooling for girls!" she urged.

In 1778, Abigail thought that John might at last come home. Instead, Congress appointed him Commissioner of France, where he helped negotiate a peace treaty after the British were defeated in 1781. After that, he stayed as the American ambassador to France.

For eight long years Abigail and John lived apart, and that was too long. From Braintree, Abigail wrote, "Hope and fear have been the two ruling passions of . . . my life. I have been bandied from one to the other like a tennis ball. Life is too short to have the dearest enjoyment curtailed . . . Give me the man I love!" From Paris, John replied as passionately, "I must go to you or you must come to me. I cannot live in this horrid solitude." In 1784, Abigail at last sailed for France. John, awaiting her arrival, boasted to a friend, "My amiable lady has earned the good title of heroine."

The heroine accompanied John to five diplomatic posts around the world, championing women's rights and women's education all the while. In 1789, John became vice president of the United States. In 1796 he was elected the nation's second President. The task was so daunting that John confessed to his first lady, "I never wanted your advice and assistance more in my life!"

In her last years, Abigail kept giving that advice to John, and to her oldest son John Quincy Adams, who became a U.S. Congressman. Abigail died in 1818, and seven years later, in 1825, her son became the sixth American president. That makes Abigail Adams the only American woman to be both a wife and a mother of U.S. presidents. But Abigail Adams deserves a greater place in history than "wife and mother of great men"! After her death, an admiring grandson published her letters, and something awesome happened. They were a hit—in that generation, and the next, and the next. Abigail Adams's inspirational life and ideas made her a household name. And her words, "Remember the Ladies!" became the rallying cry for generations of women who followed in her footsteps.

★ ★ ★ ★ ★ ★ ★ ★ ★ ★ ★ ★ ★ ★ ★ ★ ★ ★

FEMALE SEMINARIES

Abigail Adams wasn't alone in promoting better education for females after the war. Girls' boarding schools called seminaries were all the rage. By the 1790s nearly a hundred seminaries operated in America. To promote female education, Abigail and other women used a foolproof argument even conservative men couldn't dispute: Educating females is in the best interest of males, whose first teachers are women—their mothers. "If we mean to have heroes, statesmen, and philosophers," Abigail said, "we should have learned women!"

★ ★ ★ ★ ★ ★ ★ ★ ★ ★ ★ ★ ★ ★ ★ ★ ★ ★

Phillis Wheatley

(1 7 5 3   –   1 7 8 4)

Imagine being torn from your parents' arms and thrown into the hot, stinky bowels of a slave ship with hundreds of terrified strangers. That was the harrowing fate of a frail 7-year-old girl from western Africa in 1761. Yet 10 years after her arrival at Boston's Feather Wharf, this extraordinary child had become a published poet and international celebrity!

The slave child's amazing transformation began on a chilly June day in Boston. Well-dressed white men and women milled about the shivering child, who was covered only in a scrap of cloth. They clutched flyers advertising the sale of "rum, tobacco and likely Negroes." Scrawny Phillis was *not* a good buy, though. Most of the slave shoppers didn't even give her a second glance, for they wanted "breeders" of childbearing age. However, one 52-year-old saw the small slave girl and thought, "The poor little outcast! I'll take her home and mold her into a good Christian lady's maid and

THE GREAT AWAKENING

Religion drew many people to the American colonies and the "Great Awakening" of the mid 1700s, a period of religious renewal, helped fuel the American Revolution. During the Great Awakening, fire-and-brimstone preachers encouraged heartfelt religious conversion or "new birth."

The passionate preacher George Whitefield inspired much of this conversion. He traveled on horseback throughout the colonies—and spoke the language of the heart. After hearing him, people spoke of wanting to dance for joy. They believed in the Kingdom of God on Earth—and on American shores!

Thanks to the Great Awakening, the ranks of Presbyterians, Baptists, and Methodists swelled, while Anglicans, Quakers, and Congregationalists were left in the dust. Because conversion was available to all races, classes, and genders, many barriers among people crumbled. Soon the converted were declaring that Jesus was their only king (not that pretender on the throne in England!).

★ ★ ★ ★ ★ ★ ★ ★ ★ ★ ★ ★ ★ ★ ★ ★ ★ ★

companion." Mrs. Wheatley paid the slaver a few pounds, named the child Phillis, after the boat she arrived on, and took her home.

Home was a big house on busy King Street. Phillis—who did not speak a lick of English—was bathed, dressed in a clean cotton gown, and fed a bountiful meal. Later, Phillis Wheatley understood that she was owned—like a chair, or a carriage, or a dog. For a very long time, however, she knew only one thing: Susannah Wheatley was an angel who had plucked her out of hell.

★ ★ ★ ★ ★ ★ ★ ★ ★ ★ ★ ★ ★ ★ ★ ★ ★ ★

Of course, Susannah Wheatley wasn't an angel, but her religious beliefs did lead her to treat her slaves well. This wife of a successful Boston merchant believed that blacks were meant by God to be "servants of servants." Nonetheless she had also been swept up in a movement called the Great Awakening. Like others influenced by the movement, Susannah Wheatley believed that slaves who converted to Christianity would become equal to whites in heaven.

For Phillis to become a Christian, Mrs. Wheatley first had to teach her to read the Bible. The Wheatley family discovered that Phillis was brilliant and famished for learning. By the time she was 10, Phillis was reading everything in the house—newspapers, poetry, novels, astronomy, mythology, you name it. By the time she was 12, Phillis could read and write Greek and Latin. And by the time she was 13, she'd written her first poem.

Susannah Wheatley acted like a proud parent, stage mother, and literary agent all rolled into one. A big portrait of Phillis hung above the Wheatleys' living-room mantle. In it, Phillis sat at a desk holding a quill pen over a piece of paper. In her frilly white cap and dainty gown, she looked demure, obedient, and delicate.

Mrs. Wheatley put a candle, inkwell, and quill pen by Phillis's bedside at night, in case she woke and was inspired to write in the wee hours. Phillis was inspired, but the words that flowed from her pen weren't always demure! Actually, Phillis wrote two very different kinds of poems. Some were very religious, and Susannah Wheatley sent these to newspapers and magazines that published them. But other poems were about the revolutionary events unfolding outside Phillis's bedroom window. She wrote, "the power of liberty makes the weak strong." She wrote about Redcoats landing and a frenzied mob trashing the royal governor's mansion. When 11-year-old Christopher Snider was killed in a street-corner fight over British taxes, she wrote a poem honoring him as the "first martyr for the common good."

Writing poems praising revolutionaries showed Phillis had gumption, because Susannah Wheatley's husband did not like the "rebel horde." His attitude probably explains why most of Phillis's pro-Patriot poems were never published—and later disappeared. John Wheatley probably pitched a fit and threw them into the drawing-room fire!

It was Phillis's religious poems, not her political ones, that first made her popular among the Boston elite. What Susannah Wheatley taught, Phillis bought—hook, line, and sinker. "Negroes, black as Cain, will someday join the angelic train," she wrote.

A DEMURE LOOKING PHILLIS PONDERS HER MUSE.

★ ★ ★ ★ ★ ★ ★ ★ ★ ★ ★ ★ ★ ★ ★ ★ ★ ★ ★

PHILLIS WHEATLEY'S POETRY

Phillis's first published poem, which appeared in the *Newport Mercury*, told a story Phillis had heard about two ship captains who had nearly shipwrecked off the coast of Cape Cod. Not long after that, Phillis wrote one of her few poems that mention Africa. In "On Being Brought from Africa to America," 15-year-old Phillis wrote she was grateful for having been enslaved—and "saved."

> 'Twas mercy brought me from my Pagan land,
> Taught my benighted soul to understand,
> That there's a God, that there's a savior, too.

★ ★ ★ ★ ★ ★ ★ ★ ★ ★ ★ ★ ★ ★ ★ ★ ★ ★ ★

At 19, Phillis she got her big break with one of these religious poems. She wrote an elegy—poem praising the dead—about Great Awakening superstar minister, Reverend George White-field. Phillis's elegy was all the rage in Boston, Philadelphia, New York, and London. In England, the Countess of Huntingdon read the poem and invited Phillis to come to England and publish a book of her poetry.

It took some serious persuading for Susannah Wheatley to agree to let Phillis go. But in 1773, Phillis walked down the gang-plank and onto London's crowded wharf. Before long, the pretty slave poet was the talk of the town. In Boston, Susannah Wheat-ley's friends tended to treat Phillis like some exotic animal in the zoo. They praised her poetry, but when dinnertime rolled around, Phillis ate at a small table set for her alone. Talent or no, she re-mained inferior—in this life if not the next!

But Londoners, however, were a different kettle of fish. The antislavery movement in England had gained greater force than in the American colonies, and a steady stream of prominent activists visited her lodgings. Phillis was completely bowled over when London's antislavery movement leaders asked for her opinions, dined by her side, and said she should be free! Phillis worked on her book, soaked up their ideas, and basked in their admiration.

With the countess in her corner and her book due off the presses any day, Phillis was floating on cloud nine—but the young poet's bliss wouldn't last. After only a month in London, word ar-rived that Susannah Wheatley was dying. "I know you are eager to stay in London," her mistress wrote. "But I need you by my side. Please come home!"

Phillis returned to Boston to nurse her mistress, who died several months later. Meanwhile, reviews of her book hit the London newspapers. Proslavery reviewers found *Poems, on Various Subjects, Religious and Moral* abominable. But antislavery advocates treated the book like a gift from God. "This book proves that liberty-loving Americans are a bunch of hypocrites," the reviewers wrote. "Even a blind man on a galloping horse can see that cries of freedom mean nothing if Phillis Wheatley, and other Africans, remain enslaved!"

Susannah Wheatley's death and the publication of Phillis's book won Phillis her freedom and changed her life forever. Phillis was freed, probably as her mistress lay on her deathbed. This sounds like a wonderful happy ending, doesn't it? Sadly, however, it really wasn't. Susannah Wheatley may have been a slaveholder, but she was also the poet's greatest advocate and friend. "She loved me tenderly, more like a daughter than a servant," Phillis wrote to a friend.

Phillis was free, 21 years old, and the author of a book selling like hot cross buns in London. But hard times loomed around the corner. A week after a shipment of her books arrived in America, 5,000 Redcoats arrived and shut down Boston Harbor. Ten thousand Bostonians fled the city, including the Wheatleys. Phillis may have been free, but she had no way to survive on her own. With no other choice, she fled the city with the Wheatley family and remained a dependent in their household.

On the surface, it seemed as though Phillis's relationship with the Wheatleys hadn't changed—but it had. Now she promoted her own writing and refused to be muzzled about American—and black—freedom. "In every human breast, God has implanted a principle, which we call love of freedom," Phillis wrote. "American colonists are impatient of oppression and pant for deliverance. The same principle lives in slaves."

This love of freedom apparently inspired Phillis to take charge of her own life, for after the British evacuated Boston in 1776, she struck out on her own for that war-torn city. What a sight Phillis encountered there! Cannonballs had shattered the Wheatley mansion, and the Old South Church's hand-carved pews had been turned into hog pens. Staying with friends, Phillis kept writing poems, including one praising General George Washington:

> Proceed, great chief, with virtue on thy side,
> Thy every action let the goddess guide.
> A crown, a mansion, and a throne that shine,
> With gold unfading, Washington! Be thine!

Flattered by the published poem, Washington invited the author to visit him at army headquarters in Cambridge. The slave-owning commander hadn't realized she was black and was startled. Nonetheless, she visited with him privately for a half hour, and he was impressed. (Who knows, when Washington later freed his own slaves in his will, maybe thoughts of talented Phillis Wheatley flitted into his mind.)

After her big moment with General Washington, Phillis was flying high. That's good to know, because what followed next was tragic. Boston was in shambles, and no one seemed interested in publishing poetry. John Wheatley died in 1778 and left her no money. His daughter died, too, and his Loyalist son fled to

England and forgot all about Phillis. She had been a slave, the star attraction of Boston, and the toast of London. Now that she was free, however, she was alone and penniless in a war-torn nation. Phillis did what most single colonial women did when desperate for support—she got married.

John Peters, the free black man Phillis married, was well off and handsome. John wore a white wig, carried a gold-tipped cane, and worked as a merchant and lawyer in the black community of Boston. At first, he and Phillis lived a high life in a fine brick house. All too soon, however, the two babies Phillis bore died as infants, and John fell deeply into debt. By 1784, he was in prison for debt, and Phillis was working in a seedy boarding house, with a third baby by her side. Phillis was only 31, but she'd never been healthy. Some historians think she (and her babies) probably had tuberculosis. In the end, Phillis's life was as tragic as it was remarkable. Alone, in bed, she and her third baby died, and strangers carried their bodies to an unmarked grave in an unknown location.

Despite her sad end, Phillis Wheatley was not forgotten! Generations of Americans that followed passed her poems and letters from hand to hand. Many were awed by her brilliance, angered by the injustice she suffered, and inspired to join the battle against slavery and racial inequality. When the antislavery movement heated up in America and England, people shouted from the rooftops, "The poetic talents of Phillis Wheatley prove that blacks are not an inferior race." One British antislavery activist railed at Parliament, "If Phillis Wheatley was designed for slavery, then British people should lose their freedom, too!"

Part Two

★ ★ ★ ★ ★ ★ ★ ★ ★ ★ ★

THE MIDDLE COLONIES

COMPARED TO NEW ENGLAND *and the southern colonies, the middle colonies were diverse, tolerant, and sophisticated. On the streets of Quaker-dominated Philadelphia and Anglican-dominated New York, many languages were spoken. Successful businesses created thriving colonial centers. In the fertile Pennsylvania countryside, people of German, Scottish, and Irish descent ran small farms and cottage industries such as spinning and cabinetmaking. In the New York countryside, people from all over Europe mingled freely. In Maryland, religious tolerance and diversity also developed early, although there, as in the southern colonies, wealthy aristocrats had huge tobacco plantations that depended on slave labor.*

★ ★ ★ ★ ★ ★ ★ ★ ★ ★

Margaret Brent

(1601 - 1671)

H ad she been born a queen, she would have been as brilliant and daring as Elizabeth!" That's what writer John Thomas thought of Maryland businesswoman and politician Margaret Brent.

Born in 1601 to a Catholic family of Gloucestershire, Scotland, Margaret fled to Maryland to escape religious persecution against Catholics by militant Puritans. As Catholic members of the gentry, Margaret's parents risked having their entire estate confiscated. The Brents also had 13 children, so it was important that some of them find their fortunes elsewhere! The colony of Maryland, founded a few years earlier as a refuge for Catholics, seemed a good bet.

On a chilly November day in 1638, Margaret sailed up the Potomac River with her sister Mary and her brothers Giles and Fulke. Margaret carried a letter from the colony's landowner, Lord Baltimore (Cecil Calvert) to his brother, the colony's governor. Only five years before, the first settlers had arrived in the colony

★ ★ ★ ★ ★ ★ ★ ★ ★ ★ ★ ★ ★ ★ ★ ★ ★ ★

granted to the Calvert family by Charles I. "Sell the worthy Brent siblings grants of land on favorable terms," the letter read, and Governor Leonard Calvert obeyed.

As a single woman, Margaret was a rare breed. For every single woman among Maryland's 500 souls, there were six wife-hunting men! Nonetheless, Margaret and her sister Mary reveled in their independence. Their 70-acre tobacco plantation in St. Mary's City was proudly named Sisters Freehold. Along with it, Margaret also had 1,000 acres on Kent Island.

Margaret became a respected Maryland businesswoman. She gave the overseer his daily orders, imported indentured servants, registered cattle marks, loaned money to incoming settlers, and raised tobacco for export. In court, she handled her own business and legal affairs. Other single women depended on male relatives for such things, but Margaret did fine on her own. In fact, she often acted as her brothers' representative in court, too. Margaret's unique status stumped the men at court. Unsure how to address such an independent woman, they came up with an odd solution. In official records, Margaret was called, "Gentleman Margaret Brent"!

In 1645, an English civil war between Catholics and Protestants spilled over onto Maryland's shores. A Protestant ship from

★ ★ ★ ★ ★ ★ ★ ★ ★ ★ ★ ★ ★ ★ ★ ★ ★ ★

WOMEN AND THE LAW

Under English law, single and widowed women could sue in court, sign contracts, and control their own property. Once a woman married, however, she had the same rights as children, criminals, and the insane—none. Any property a woman owned—clothes, land, books, jewels—became her husband's to do with as he pleased. (Maybe that's why Margaret Brent chose to stay single!)

★ ★ ★ ★ ★ ★ ★ ★ ★ ★ ★ ★ ★ ★ ★ ★ ★ ★

England attacked Maryland, looted the estates of the wealthier Catholics, and briefly seized control of the colony's government. Historians call it Ingles Rebellion after the captain of the ship. Marylanders called it, "The Time of Troubles." Life got so hairy during the short-lived rebellion that three quarters of the population fled to more peaceful neighboring colonies.

Governor Calvert—one colonist called him a hearty, rattling, wild young dog of an officer—fled to Virginia. In Virginia, the exiled governor hired mercenary (privately paid) soldiers to help him win back Maryland. Calvert wanted to keep Maryland a haven for Catholics and to regain power, but he had a big problem: no cash to pay the soldiers. To remedy that, Governor Calvert pledged to pay them later out of his own pocket. The soldiers agreed and put down the Protestant revolt, and Calvert and his allies returned to power. Right after that, though, the governor grew deathly ill. When the restless Virginia soldiers learned of this, they demanded their money—and threatened to attack if they didn't get it!

On his deathbed, Leonard Calvert named Thomas Green to be governor. But he entrusted the settlement of his personal estate to a prominent land owner and his good friend (some say secret love), Margaret Brent. This caused a huge uproar, of course. First, Margaret was a mere woman! Also, everyone had expected that Lord Baltimore, who was back in England, would be named executor. Governor Calvert knew, however, that Maryland was in deep, immediate trouble. He wanted someone wise, loyal, and *local* to take matters quickly in hand. "I make you the only manager of my estate," Governor Calvert told Margaret on his deathbed. "Collect my debts. Settle my legal cases. Pay the soldiers. Save Maryland!"

★ ★ ★ ★ ★ ★ ★ ★ ★ ★ ★ ★ ★ ★ ★ ★ ★ ★

WORKING WOMEN

Margaret Brent wasn't the only colonial businesswoman. Colonial house-wives often made money to add to the family income—trading cheese and candles for lumber and seeds, or earning money by spinning, weaving, knit-ting, baking, midwifery, and teaching. Other women worked outside the home more than in it—as servants, tradeswomen, doctors, cobblers, shop-keepers, and publishers.

In the printing trade, women were especially common. Wives worked alongside husbands and sons—setting type, writing editorials, binding books, and more. Then when their husbands died, the women carried on alone.

★ ★ ★ ★ ★ ★ ★ ★ ★ ★ ★ ★ ★ ★ ★ ★ ★ ★ ★

Margaret, then 46, was determined to do just that. She moved into Calvert's mansion, set up a headquarters, and invento-ried all of his property and accounts. With a cool hand, she began to sell off his entire estate.

Whipping Maryland back into shape was no easy task. In ad-dition to soldiers clamoring for their pay, people were threatening to riot over a shortage of food. Margaret came through with flying colors to solve these problems: She paid Calvert's debts, she paid the soldiers, and to ease the food shortage, she imported wag-onloads of food from Virginia.

Governor Calvert had been the manager of Lord Baltimore's property in Maryland, so Margaret had control of that, too. When she'd spent all of Calvert's money and needed more, Margaret didn't hesitate to dip into the powerful absentee landlord's coffer. Without even asking permission, she sold his cattle. Thanks to Margaret's swift actions, order was restored.

To preserve Maryland as a safe place for Catholics, the new governor quickly made moves to appease the Protestants by passing a Toleration Act that allowed freedom of worship for all faiths. Margaret Brent didn't fare so well in the new Maryland, however. Although many of the colony's leaders praised Margaret's actions, she still had enemies in the Maryland Assembly. Outraged muck-a-mucks challenged her authority to be Calvert and Baltimore's agent, and although the courts upheld her rights Margaret decided she could only exert full influence as Calvert's representative if she had the right to vote. She decided to obtain the dead Governor Leonard Calvert's two votes in the Maryland Assembly (one for himself and one for his brother Lord Baltimore). It was the first time on American soil that a woman sought such a right.

On January 21, 1648, Margaret heard the drumbeat that called the assembly together. On horseback, she headed to Fort St. Johns and addressed the assembly. "As agent for Leonard Calvert and Lord Baltimore, I demand two votes in this Assembly," she proclaimed. All too soon, Margaret learned she had more enemies than friends—including Lord Baltimore back in England. He'd sent word from England that Margaret Brent should be stopped. The assembly informed Margaret, "Lord Baltimore is displeased by your meddling in his affairs. He sends word that you should receive no votes and that you must relinquish control of the Calvert estates."

★ ★ ★ ★ ★ ★ ★ ★ ★ ★ ★ ★ ★ ★ ★ ★ ★ ★

Lord Baltimore had ended Margaret's glorious reign of power. By 1651, her enemies had forced her to flee to the Northern Neck region of Virginia. There she bought land, brought in dozens of settlers from England, and built a new plantation named Peace. When Margaret died there in 1671, her lucky nieces and nephews inherited a thriving estate. Today, in St. Mary's City, Maryland, a memorial depicts the scene where "Gentleman Margaret Brent" asked the assembly for the right to vote.

★ ★ ★ ★ ★ ★ ★ ★ ★ ★ ★

Peggy Shippen Arnold

(1 7 6 0 – 1 8 0 4)

W hen a swarm of Redcoats chased the American Patriots out of Philadelphia in the fall of 1777, residents fled in droves. Wagons of refugees clogged the narrow roads, and the Continental Congress trotted off to Lancaster, Pennsylvania. General George Washington's army was in retreat, and 17-year-old Peggy Shippen clapped her hands gleefully. She could hardly wait to hit the dance floor with a slough of handsome and elegant British officers.

When Peggy Shippen was born on June 11, 1760, her father said that his last child was welcome—despite its being "the worst sex." How shocked he would have been if someone had suggested that his pretty pampered Peggy would grow up to become the highest paid spy of the American Revolution!

As a child, Peggy and her family lived in a dazzling mansion on Philadelphia's Society Hill. A spacious lawn shaded by ancient elm and linden trees separated the family from the city's wide

★ ★ ★ ★ ★ ★ ★ ★ ★ ★ ★ ★ ★ ★ ★ ★ ★ ★

streets. In her protected palace, Peggy spent her days with tutors who gave lessons in speaking French, singing ballads, dancing the minuet, reading, and writing. By her teen years, her lazy afternoons were set aside for chaperoned drawing-room visits with eligible gentlemen callers. Peggy's famous delicate beauty—golden curls, creamy skin, and rosebud mouth—drew scads of admirers.

Brewing hostilities with England disrupted Peggy's charmed life, however. Peggy's father, a powerful judge, thought Parliament's new laws crushed native talents and industries. Nonetheless the judge was horrified that "the common sort" was suddenly demanding to be treated as equals. Judge Shippen tried hard to straddle the political fence, but that became tricky. "Poor America!" Peggy often heard him moan. "It has seen its best days."

By 1776, America had declared independence, and the Shippens couldn't hide from the war anymore. Philadelphia's leading patriots threatened to seize the Shippens' home and other properties if Peggy's father didn't sign an oath of loyalty to the Ameri-

★ ★ ★ ★ ★ ★ ★ ★ ★ ★ ★ ★ ★ ★ ★ ★ ★ ★ ★

THE CITY OF BROTHERLY LOVE

Philadelphia was so hot, muggy, buggy, and grimy that a visiting French diplomat remarked, "At each inhaling of air, one worries about the next one." Horse dung, dust, and swarms of insects filled the streets, and slop filled the gutters. Housewives and maids tried valiantly to defeat the dirt— cleaning window ledges, doors, and sidewalks twice a week—but it was a losing battle. Despite this, the unofficial capital of the colonies was the happening hub of political, social, and business life.

★ ★ ★ ★ ★ ★ ★ ★ ★ ★ ★ ★ ★ ★ ★ ★ ★ ★ ★

can cause. The judge didn't want to sign. "Those hot-headed idiots have a lot of gall!" he muttered then quickly whisked his startled family off to the boondocks of New Jersey. Perhaps, he hoped, no one would bother them there.

Peggy endured her exile in the sticks impatiently—until the British occupied Philadelphia in 1777. The British required no such oath of loyalty—but they did burn down vacant mansions of absent Philadelphians and turned others into stables. The Shippens scurried back home to protect their property and see what the British were all about.

When Peggy saw that the British invasion was transforming the city into a mini-London, she was thrilled! Elegant red-coated officers hosted balls more extravagant than Philadelphia had ever seen. French silk stockings, diamond necklaces, and gold-tipped canes were all the rage. Hairstyles—a woman's crowning glory—grew to be two-foot-tall masterpieces that took hours to create and forced women to ride with their heads sticking out of carriage windows!

That winter, while Washington and his men froze and starved at nearby Valley Forge, river barges strung with lights became floating dance floors. Laughing groups of young people wrapped in bearskin rugs raced down snow-covered hills on giant sleds. At gala dinners, men dressed as gallant medieval knights, with the society belles as their fair maidens. Each one tried to be more glamorous than the next, and Peggy was a huge success at that. Other society belles wrote in their diaries, "All the young men are in love with Peggy."

One dashing officer, Lieutenant John Andre thought Peggy was a knockout. The flirty and accomplished young Englishman (a poet *and* an artist) sketched 17-year-old Peggy's portrait. He also gave her a locket that held a ringlet of his hair. The romance did not seem to go anywhere, but the pretty pair became fast friends.

When the British withdrew to New York in May 1778, hundreds of Loyalists fled with them. Despite all their hobnobbing with the British brass, however, Peggy's family still hoped to remain neutral. They stayed to greet the new American military governor of Philadelphia. General George Washington gave the post to a wounded war hero who needed some time away from the battle to heal a badly wounded leg. I'm sure you've heard of the gen-

★ ★ ★ ★ ★ ★ ★ ★ ★ ★ ★ ★ ★ ★ ★ ★ ★ ★

A BIG BRITISH BASH

Just before they left Philadelphia in 1778, the British held a lavish costume ball with a special theme: *The Ancient Age of Chivalry.*

Peggy Shippen, her sisters, and 40 other Philly belles attended. All dolled up in Turkish harem pants, spangled turbans, flowing tunics, and silk sashes, they were escorted to the ball on barges decorated with ribbons and roses. Bands serenaded them, and British ships fired their guns in salute as they passed!

At the mansion where the party was held, there was dancing, fireworks, and supper in a 200-foot-long mirror-lined dining hall. On the long table were 1,200 dishes served by two dozen servants in oriental dress. After dinner, a trumpeter blew his horn, and everyone sang "God Save the King."

★ ★ ★ ★ ★ ★ ★ ★ ★ ★ ★ ★ ★ ★ ★ ★ ★ ★

eral, for with Peggy's help he became America's most famous traitor. His name was Benedict Arnold.

General Arnold was famous for his daring feats in battle when he rode into town in a gold-trimmed coach pulled by six fine horses. (Even George Washington didn't travel in such style.) The public lined the streets, cheering him on, as befitted a conquering war hero. Before long, however, Patriot leaders hated him with a passion. They had expected Arnold to fine, jail, even hang Philadelphians who had welcomed the British—and were furious when he did not. Instead of punishing "collaborators," Arnold invited them to his own elaborate balls and parties. Peggy, of course, approved. Arnold invited the famous beauty to his parties, and soon she was whispering sweet nothings to him. "You can't believe how fond of kissing she is," Sarah Franklin told her father Ben. "General Arnold says she should be a school-mistress and teach all the young ladies how to kiss."

Was Peggy swept off her feet by the rugged-looking widower 20 years her senior? Was she attracted to his great wealth and powerful position? Or was it a little of both? Peggy's family later destroyed her personal letters, so we may never know. We do know this, however: The Shippen family fortune was suffering because of the war, Arnold was rich, and Peggy had a fondness for the luxuries money could buy!

Soon hard-boiled Patriots were accusing General Arnold of crimes against the Continental Army. Patriots said that, along with befriending Loyalists, he stole flour and other supplies from the army, then sold the scarce goods to the highest bidder and pocketed the profits (called profiteering). Peggy stood by her man. "He's as innocent as a new born baby!" she cooed. Then she married him.

★ ★ ★ ★ ★ ★ ★ ★ ★ ★ ★ ★ ★ ★ ★ ★ ★ ★

Shady things happened with lightning speed after Peggy tied the knot with Benedict Arnold. In May of 1779, Pennsylvania leaders officially charged Peggy's husband with profiteering, and a military court found him guilty. Surprising as it sounds, though, selling army supplies on the sly was common practice then, so this conviction was no huge deal. Also, Washington still felt that Arnold's military skills were needed to help win the war. For those reasons, the court sentenced Arnold to only a formal reprimand. In a public letter, George Washington did the scolding, then to show there were no hard feelings, he wrote privately to the Arnolds. In this second letter, the commander-in-chief congratulated them on the birth of their first child—and offered Arnold a place as his number-two general!

Benedict Arnold sure had gotten off easy (some said Scot-free), but he and Peggy didn't think so. Washington's offer of a high command did not soothe their ruffled feathers. "They don't appreciate me," Arnold complained to Peggy, "but perhaps the British will." The British, in fact, did. Within a month of their marriage, the couple began betraying their country.

By 1780, Peggy had joined her husband as a full partner in crime. She secretly got in touch with her old British pal, John Andre, now a major and the head honcho of British Intelligence. Andre thought it was just dandy that the Arnolds wanted to "turn coat." He especially respected Peggy, and told the messenger who carried the spy ring's coded letters, "Deal with the lady."

The lady had no problem with that! She devised clever schemes for hiding the couple's spying activities. In her bedroom, she received and delivered military secrets using codes and invisible ink.

The Arnolds told Andre about troop movements and the number of weapons the Americans had. The information led to successful British attacks on New York and on Charleston, South Carolina. The dynamic duo didn't stop there, however. Encouraged by their success, Peggy and her husband hatched a deadly plot to seriously weaken the Continental Army.

West Point, up the Hudson River from New York City, was their target. The New York fort was one of a string of important posts that ran from Manhattan to Lake Champlain. If the British could take it, victory would be theirs. To set the plot in motion, Benedict Arnold wrote to General Washington and asked for the command of West Point. Washington agreed.

Spies get paid, of course, and the Arnolds named their price. For turning over West Point, the British promised them a fortune—20,000 pounds. Not only that, Benedict and Peggy Arnold would become a duke and duchess! That was a juicy incentive for the socially ambitious pair.

★ ★ ★ ★ ★ ★ ★ ★ ★ ★ ★ ★ ★ ★ ★ ★ ★

DARING DAMSEL SPIES AND COURIERS

Many men thought women couldn't understand military strategy and therefore posed no danger. That was a mistake! There were women spies and messengers galore—on both sides. Spying for the British with Peggy Arnold was Anne Bates, a Philadelphia schoolteacher. She disguised herself as a peddler and wandered through American camps counting the weapons and troops.

On the American side, Philadelphia nurse, midwife, and undertaker Lydia Darragh listened through a keyhole while British officers boarding in her home planned their strategies. She then sewed messages into buttons and sewing needle packets and smuggled them to Washington's headquarters.

★ ★ ★ ★ ★ ★ ★ ★ ★ ★ ★ ★ ★ ★ ★ ★ ★

By September 1780, Peggy and Benedict Arnold, with their new infant son, were at the fort. A few weeks later, George Washington sent word that he would come inspect the troops. The excited Arnolds thought they saw their chance. They would capture George Washington himself (what a prize!). Then they'd notify a British warship anchored downriver to attack. They reasoned that the Americans would be so weakened and humiliated after that, they would throw in the towel.

The day of Washington's visit, Peggy paced before a window upstairs. Benedict and his staff were eating breakfast downstairs when a mud-splattered messenger dashed in. Andre had been captured just north of Tarry Town that morning, he announced breathlessly. A group of American soldiers looking for Loyalists had stopped and stripped Andre down to his underwear. In his socks they found papers that revealed the Arnolds' plot. "This is a spy!" one surprised soldier shouted, and they hauled John Andre back to camp.

The Arnolds knew the plot was foiled. Damning evidence would soon be in Washington's hands. Benedict sprinted up the stairs to tell Peggy. Because her part wasn't revealed in Andre's papers, Peggy agreed to stay at West Point with their son and put up a show of innocence. As soon as her husband escaped, Peggy poured on the hysterics. She pulled pins from her mass of blond curls, clutched her baby to her chest, and ran through the upstairs hall in her nightgown. When servants rushed to help, she screeched like a banshee and shoved them wildly aside. When Benedict's officers rushed upstairs, Peggy grabbed one and cried. "My husband is dead, dead, dead. Have you ordered my child to be killed, too?! Then she fell to her knees, wrapped her dainty arms around the officers' legs and cried, "I cannot bear such shame. Please spare my innocent babe!"

When Washington arrived, he sent men to chase the long-gone Arnold, then he went upstairs to question Peggy. As soon as she saw Washington, the hysterical Peggy wailed, "That is not George Washington. That is the man who is going to kill my child!" Alexander Hamilton, an officer with Washington, was very touched by poor Peggy's pain. "Her sufferings were so eloquent that I wished to become her defender," wrote the gallant Hamilton. "If I could forgive Arnold for sacrificing his honor, reputation, and duty, I could not forgive him for losing the respect of so fine a woman."

MAJOR ANDRE MADE THIS SKETCH OF HIMSLEF THE MORNING OF HIS EXECUTION.

Peggy was a fine actress, for Washington was as duped as Hamilton. Both believed that innocent Peggy had been betrayed and deceived by a wicked man. Washington sent Peggy and her baby back to her family in Philadelphia. Meanwhile, Benedict arrived safely in New York, where the British made him a Brigadier General—and John Andre was convicted of spying and hanged.

Unfortunately for Peggy, Pennsylvanians knew she was a wolf in sheep's clothing and promptly evicted her from the state. She traveled to her husband in New York, and before long, they both sailed for England. At the Royal Court, Peggy, only 22, was a smash hit, and her popularity served her well. She had four more boys, who grew up and got plush appointments as British officers, and a daughter who grew up and married an officer. Moneywise, Peggy cleaned up, too. For her spying services, she was paid 1,000

★ ★ ★ ★ ★ ★ ★ ★ ★ ★ ★ ★ ★ ★ ★ ★ ★

Courtesy of North Wind Picture Archives

pounds a year for life, as well as tidy sums for her children. For his spying, Benedict Arnold got only a one-time payment of 6,350 pounds. This means that Peggy was the highest paid British spy of the American Revolution—not her notorious husband. Despite this, Benedict Arnold became an archvillain for all time, and Peggy Arnold was pitied as a poor duped victim for a hundred years! It wasn't until the late 1900s that newly discovered British military papers firmly proved her involvement.

When Peggy died of cancer at age 44, her family members back in Philadelphia still busily defended her as the wronged wife (some truly thought her innocent). In contrast, Philadelphia Patriots of the time vividly remembered her candlelit trysts with John Andre, and they learned a powerful lesson about women. A newspaper editor wrote, "Mrs. Arnold's actions prove it is very dangerous to believe that female opinions are of no consequence in public matters. Behold the consequences!"

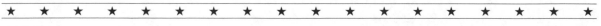

★ ★ ★ ★ ★ ★ ★ ★ ★ ★ ★

CHAPTER 9

Betsy Griscom Ross

(1 7 5 2 – 1 8 3 6)

Betsy Ross lived at Arch Street and Second.
Her sewing was very, very fine.
George Washington paid her a visit,
To order a brand new flag
Six white stripes and seven pretty red ones,
Thirteen stars on a field of navy blue.
'Twas the first flag our country ever floated,
Three cheers for the red, white, and blue—

Have you heard this song about the most famous woman of the American Revolution? It's a neat song, but historians are mostly divided into two camps: the majority who say Betsy Ross did not sew the first American flag—and the minority who insist she did.

It was a story told by Betsy's grandson that made Betsy the most famous woman of the American Revolution. Rather than dive

★ ★ ★ ★ ★ ★ ★ ★ ★ ★ ★ ★ ★ ★ ★ ★ ★ ★

★ ★ ★ ★ ★ ★ ★ ★ ★ ★ ★ ★ ★ ★ ★ ★ ★ ★ ★ ★

THE LEGEND OF BETSY ROSS

In 1870, nearly a century after Betsy Ross was said to have sewn the first flag, America was getting ready to celebrate its 100th birthday. Betsy's grandson, William Canby, told the Pennsylvania Historical Association a story. He said his grandmother had sewed the first American flag, at George Washington's request. Of course, everyone loved William Canby's story. For the big birthday bash they now had a poster woman of the American Revolution!

Canby had no convincing proof for his story, but everyone believed it. Because no portrait of Betsy survived, artist Charles H. Weisgerber got busy. He painted "Birth of Our Nation's Flag." The oil painting showed a dignified Widow Ross with the huge flag draped across her lap. Admiring her masterpiece are George Washington, Robert Morris, and Betsy's uncle, George Ross. These three men, according to Canby, visited Ross and asked her to sew the flag.

The painting was displayed at the Chicago World's Fair, appeared in popular magazines, and still appears in history books today. True or false, Betsy Ross lives on!

★ ★ ★ ★ ★ ★ ★ ★ ★ ★ ★ ★ ★ ★ ★ ★ ★ ★ ★ ★

into this debate, however, let's ask, Who was Betsy Ross? What was her life like? What else did she do? Would she deserve her fame even if she didn't earn her status as the Revolution's most celebrated woman?

The answer is yes! The flesh-and-blood Betsy eloped to marry the man of her choice and was banished from her Quaker meeting (congregation) for doing so. She also formed her very own religious group to support the Patriot cause, survived three husbands, and built a thriving family business from the ground up!

★ ★ ★ ★ ★ ★ ★ ★ ★ ★ ★ ★ ★ ★ ★ ★ ★ ★ ★ ★

Courtesy of the Library Company of Philadelphia

Born in 1752 on New Year's Day, Betsy was the seventh of 15 children born to Philadelphia Quakers. Betsy's father, Samuel Griscom, was a successful architect and carpenter. He helped build the bell tower of Carpenter's Hall, where in 1774 the Continental Congress met to discuss breaking away from England.

As Quakers, the Griscom family opposed all violence and war. They also had uncommon ideas about education and women's roles. Quakers educated girls and boys, and both learned marketable skills and trades. Betsy learned basic reading, writing, and arithmetic, then was apprenticed to a master upholsterer. Today, upholsterers work mostly on furniture coverings, but back then, they made everything from carpets, clothes, and lace, to flags and pouches that held gunpowder.

Betsy's parents expected her to marry a fellow Quaker. So many Quakers youths were marrying non-Quakers and switching

COLONIAL FLAGS

American colonies, militias, regiments, and ships all had their own banners. Many New England flags sported a green pine tree—native to the region—on a white background. The Continental Navy flew a flag with a coiled rattlesnake on a yellow background and sported the words, "Don't Tread on Me." The designer of the snake flag chose the snake because it never begins an attack, and once it strikes it never gives up.

★ ★ ★ ★ ★ ★ ★ ★ ★ ★ ★ ★ ★ ★ ★ ★ ★ ★ ★

to their spouse's faith that the Quakers were worried about survival of their religion. They made a firm rule: Marry a Quaker—or be booted out! Some young people obeyed the rule. Others, like Betsy, followed their hearts despite the dire consequences.

John Ross, the son of an Episcopalian minister at Christ Church, was Betsy's fellow apprentice upholsterer. He and Betsy fell in love—and eloped! On a cold November night in 1773, Betsy wrapped herself in a long wool cloak and slipped out of her house. John Ross met her, and they rode the ferry across the Delaware River. At Huggs Tavern, they married. For this, Betsy was cast out of her Quaker meeting. No one in the congregation would even speak to her, not even her own family!

Betsy and John attended Christ Church and started their own upholstery business. Two simple, rented rooms on Arch Street became their home and workshop. A decade earlier, Betsy and

John probably would have grown rich in Philadelphia's booming economy. But Quakers did not patronize the shameful young couple's business. Boycotts also interrupted trade, and supplies were hard to come by. Betsy and her young husband had a couple of rough years trying to make ends meet.

Like all colonial men between ages 16 and 60, John Ross belonged to the militia. After the Battle of Bunker Hill, his unit was activated and Betsy began managing their business alone. In 1776, while guarding munitions, John died in an accidental explosion. At age 24, Betsy was a widow. "These are the times that try men's souls," Thomas Paine wrote. He was right, and widows had it especially rough. Most inherited only a part of their husband's estates. Many inherited a pile of debts. Thanks to her schooling and training, Betsy was lucky. At least she had a profession to keep her afloat.

Betsy continued working—and founded a new Quaker sect. Betsy's new 200-member congregation, called the Free Quakers, abandoned traditional Quaker pacifism and supported the Patriot cause. Before long, Bostonians dubbed them the "Fighting Quakers."

In late summer, Betsy heard that the British had conquered New York—and were headed to Philadelphia. The Continental Congress and Rebel leaders fled to avoid being arrested. Residents fled to avoid shelling and burning. But Betsy stayed to protect her home and business from looting. It wasn't long before two British officers knocked on Betsy's door and announced she was to house and feed them—by order of King George III. Betsy had no choice and reluctantly lodged the officers.

Philadelphia came to life under British rule. Homespun came off of store shelves, and fine silks, satins, and laces from Eu-

rope replaced it. Betsy disliked the showy outfits affected by the high society folks who socialized with the British officers. The skirt hoops grew so wide that women had to sashay through doors sideways! Yet, despite Betsy's aversion to the British ways, she traded with the British. After all, prices tripled under British rule, and Betsy had to pay her rent. She trimmed hats with exotic feathers—and took her enemies' money.

After the British evacuated the city, Betsy celebrated by marrying the captain of an American ship, Joseph Ashburn. By 1780 Betsy had two daughters: Zilla, who died young, and Elizabeth. But Betsy was not lucky in love. While Joseph was sailing his ship to the West Indies to buy supplies for the Continental Army, he was captured by the British. In England, they threw him into the brutal, rat-infested Old Mill Prison. About a third to half of all the American prisoners held there died. Two years after his capture, Joseph was among the dead.

No picture survives of Betsy Ross, but you know she had to be a good catch. Every time she was widowed, some new man snatched her up. John Claypoole—a man who had been in prison with her husband Joseph—came to visit and was smitten, too. Betsy took him for her third husband, and this marriage lasted a long time. Together, Betsy and John had four more healthy daughters and built their business.

Betsy may not have sewn the first American flag, but she plotted her own course in life, founded a new religious group, survived three husbands, and built a thriving family business. Until her death, at age 84, she was red, white, and blue to the bone.

★ ★ ★ ★ ★ ★ ★ ★ ★ ★ ★

Esther DeBerdt Reed

(1 7 4 6   -   1 7 8 0)

In 1780, elegant Esther Reed, the wife of Pennsylvania's chief executive, lived in a luxurious mansion taken from a banished Loyalist. Esther was too troubled by the plight of American soldiers to enjoy her lofty status, though. American soldiers were hungry! Their clothes were in tatters! Esther decided to take the bull by the horns and launch the first women's relief effort in America.

The daughter of a prominent London "Whig," Esther was born in 1746. The English Whig party wanted more power for the British Parliament, the commoners (people who aren't members of the royalty), and the American colonists. The Tory party wanted more power for the king and the royal family. Like most Whigs, Esther admired America as a land of opportunity for people of the merchant middle class. As a cultured Londoner, however, she considered America an unrefined backwater.

In 1769, Esther married Joseph Reed, a young law student from New Jersey who was studying in London. Both 23-year-old

★ ★ ★ ★ ★ ★ ★ ★ ★ ★ ★ ★ ★ ★ ★ ★ ★ ★ ★

Esther and Joseph loved England and wanted to make it their home. Back in the colonies, however, Joseph's father became ill, so the newlyweds stood on the deck of the *Pennsylvania Packet* and watched London fade into the distance. "Our stay in the colonies will be only temporary," Joseph comforted Esther.

Philadelphia, where the Reeds settled, didn't impress Esther. It was true that street lamps—the only ones in America—lined cobblestone streets that crisscrossed neatly. Nonetheless, Esther wrote to her brother back in England, "The homes are so shabby and the women all stoop like country girls. How I miss London! How I miss you and mother!"

While Esther coped with homesickness and started a family of six children, Joseph built a successful law practice. The couple kept in close touch with prominent London friends, hoping that one might find Joseph a job, so they could return to England. Often, Esther tried to explain American attitudes to her London friends. She assured her British friends, "Americans do not want independence, only a better relationship with the Mother State."

By 1774, however, Esther had changed her tune. She no longer talked of returning to England—or of better relationships. Joseph, emerging as a Rebel leader, accepted a position as the second-in-command of the Philadelphia militia. When the British General Gage marched on Concord, Joseph joined 8,000 Philadelphians protesting at Statehouse Square. Esther knew then that war was inevitable. "The people here are determined to die or be free," she now warned her British pen pals. "There is full commitment to the Glorious Cause."

No one doubted Esther's loyalty to the Rebels' cause because she was an Englishwoman. In fact the "Daughter of Liberty" became Philadelphia's top political hostess. She welcomed congressional delegates to her home—and proudly showed them around the city that she had previously called shabby!

In June 1775, the newly appointed commander-in-chief of the Continental Army, George Washington, dined at the Reeds' house. Afterward, he and Joseph stayed up all night talking. The next day, Joseph jumped on his horse and escorted Washington to New York. Esther expected her husband back in a day or two. Instead, Joseph sent a letter saying he'd accepted a position as Washington's secretary.

Without even saying goodbye, Joseph was gone. His clients were left hanging. His family had to make do on a slashed salary. Worse than that, however, was the fear! Three times the British army neared Philadelphia, and each time, Esther had to lead her children and servants into the New Jersey no-man's-land. Neither side controlled New Jersey, but both sides roamed the dirt lanes looking for fights, looting farmhouses, and taking livestock to feed their armies.

After the British left Philadelphia in 1778, the Reed family was reunited. The war moved south, and peace descended on Philadelphia. The Reeds were grateful that their home hadn't been burned down or turned into a stable for British soldiers! It would not have mattered if it had, though. Joseph became "President" of Pennsylvania, and the Reeds got a new home—a magnificent mansion taken from a family that had stayed loyal to the British.

Philadelphians now called Esther Mrs. President, but she couldn't enjoy the peace or her new status. The behavior of the city's military commander and his pretty young wife—Benedict and Peggy Arnold—made her madder than a wet hen. In fact the two women deeply despised each other. The Arnolds hosted extravagant balls and spent army money as lavishly as the occupying British had. Esther called it "absurd and preposterous!" Meanwhile, America lost a string of important battles, and Charleston, South Carolina, fell to the British. American soldiers froze, starved, and died.

Esther knew just how hungry, ragged, penniless, and discouraged American soldiers were. Some soldiers had not been paid and lost their land because they couldn't pay their taxes; others went home on leave and were jailed for debt. Although she was pregnant with her sixth child and had just recovered from smallpox, Esther was determined to act. "Society expects the tender sex to leave public matters to men," she told Joseph. "But society is wrong! I must do something to help."

The first thing Esther did was publish a newspaper article titled, "Sentiments of an American Woman." Esther wrote that it was time for women to serve the public good. "Joan of Arc, Esther of the Bible and the great European queens helped save their countries," she wrote. "American women also have a duty to serve." Esther's radical words caused an uproar. Some thought them laughable, but kindred spirits were inspired. With the latter, Esther formed the first women's relief organization in America. The Philadelphia women called it, simply, The Association.

THE SUFFERING AT VALLEY FORGE INSPIRED ESTHER TO TAKE ACTION.

★ ★ ★ ★ ★ ★ ★ ★ ★ ★ ★ ★ ★ ★ ★ ★ ★ ★

WASHINGTON
INSISTED THAT
SOLDIERS NEEDED
SHIRTS—NOT
SHILLINGS—SO
ESTHER AND HER
COHORTS PLIED
THEIR NEEDLES.

Esther and the other women planned a door-to-door fund-raising campaign unlike any America had ever seen. In pairs, the women knocked on almost every door in the city of 24,000 residents. When people answered, the women asked for money to help the Continental soldiers.

The campaign raised a whopping $300,000. A proud Esther wrote to General Washington and told him the women wanted to give the poorest soldiers cash bonuses. Washington responded with thanks but suggested that Esther instead buy cloth and sew new uniform shirts. Disappointed, Esther held her ground and wrote again to the commander-in-chief. "Would not cash boost the men's sagging morale?" she asked.

Washington, not thrilled that Esther questioned his judgment, replied, "The men would only spend the money on rum. Please trust that I know best, and do as I asked without further delay!" Outranked, Esther had no choice but to comply with Washington's wishes. The Association ladies gathered to sew 2,200 uniform shirts. Above the pocket, each shirt was embroidered with the name of the woman who had sewn it.

That August, Esther wrote to tell her husband the sewing had begun. But before Joseph could write back, Esther grew ill with dysentery—a disease bred in dirty army camps—and died.

Only 34 years old, Esther left behind five children under age eight—and thousands of half-finished shirts. Esther's friend, Benjamin Franklin's daughter Sarah Franklin Bache, made sure the shirts were finished and delivered them to George Washington. Not long after that, 2,200 American soldiers—many in lovingly hand-sewn and embroidered shirts—defeated the British at Yorktown.

★ ★ ★ ★ ★ ★ ★ ★ ★ ★ ★ ★ ★ ★ ★ ★ ★ ★

AN UNHEALTHY PLACE

Germs reigned in early America, for antibiotics didn't yet exist, and colonial folks weren't very clean (most didn't bathe all winter). That's why more soldiers died of illnesses than were killed in combat. In the dirty, cramped army camps, diseases such as the flu, smallpox, dysentery, and tuberculosis flourished. When the army marched through towns, the diseases spread to civilians. Pregnant women and infants were especially vulnerable, and many who grew ill didn't survive. One in five children died before they were a year old.

★ ★ ★ ★ ★ ★ ★ ★ ★ ★ ★ ★ ★ ★ ★ ★ ★ ★

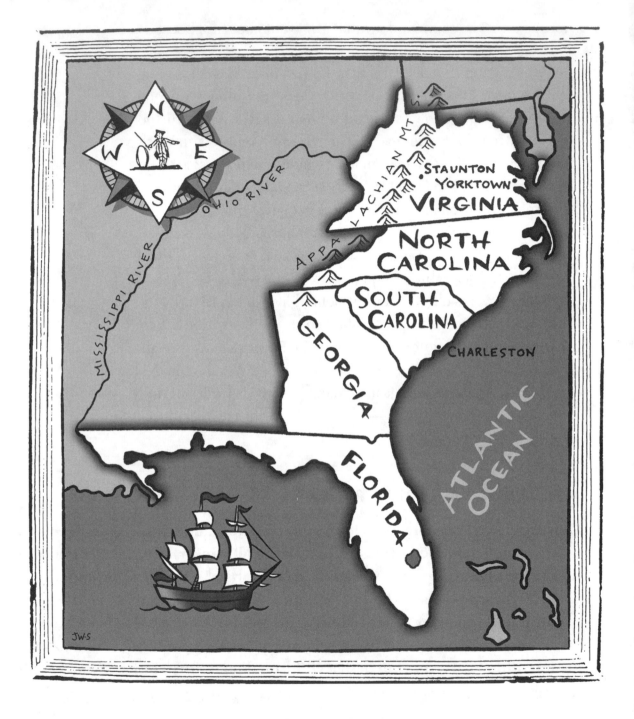

Part Three

THE SOUTH

REMOTE AND RURAL, *Virginia, North and South Carolina, and Georgia had little in common with their northern neighbors. Very wealthy planters built great mansions and lived like English aristocrats. Virginia depended on a single crop: tobacco. South Carolina and Georgia grew rice and indigo, too. Because Georgia was founded as a haven for England's poor, farms there were smaller. As in the middle colonies, German and Scotch-Irish colonists pushed west into country where Native Americans still reigned. Charleston, South Carolina, was the leading port and center of trade and commerce in the Southern colonies.*

★ ★ ★ ★ ★ ★ ★ ★ ★ ★

Anne Bonny

(1 6 9 7   –   1 7 ? ?)

Born in County Cork, Ireland, in 1697, Anne Bonny (sometimes spelled Bonney) began life in the midst of scandal, and scandal never left her. Her lawyer father, John Cormack, was respectable enough, as was his wife. Cormack's wife, however, was not Anne's mother. Mary Brennan, the family maid, had that honor. Neighborhood tongues wagged, and John Cormack's wife booted him out with his mistress and daughter. The threesome sailed off to start fresh in the colony of South Carolina.

The Cormacks settled down on a plantation, but Anne grew up wild and rebellious. As a teenager, when one young man would not stop pestering her, she thrashed him so soundly that he was bedridden for two weeks!

Despite his own disreputable past, Anne's father wasn't pleased with her shenanigans. "We're trying to be respectable, my girl. Act like a lady!" But rebellious Anne turned a deaf ear to Daddy and let a penniless soldier, James Bonny, sweep her off her feet.

★ ★ ★ ★ ★ ★ ★ ★ ★ ★ ★ ★ ★ ★ ★ ★ ★ ★ ★ ★

Unfortunately for James Bonny, Anne was a fickle lass. The luster of marriage to a poor soldier wore thin, and she took to milling about with big-spending pirates at wharfside saloons. It wasn't long before Anne caught the eye of Captain "Calico Jack" Rackam, a black-haired pirate with a fondness for pretty patchwork britches made of striped calico fabric. Calico Jack was trouble with a capital T! Murdering fiend or no, however, he had an honor code of sorts. It wasn't right to just run off with a married ladylove. He had to pay for her with gold! When Calico Jack offered to buy Anne, an outraged James Bonny protested to the South Carolina governor, who ordered Anne stripped and flogged. So much for honor codes! As fast as they could, Calico Jack and

★ ★ ★ ★ ★ ★ ★ ★ ★ ★ ★ ★ ★ ★ ★ ★ ★ ★

COLONIAL PIRATES

Charleston, the south's largest port, shipped tar, tobacco, rice, indigo, timber, and more to other colonies and to Europe. Attracted by the bounty, pirates— led by the likes of Blackbeard and William Kid—cruised the Atlantic waters in armed vessels flying black flags with skulls and crossbones. The renegade crews shared equally in all booty and were so dangerous that respectable sea captains had to know how to use weapons as well as they used winds, tides and stars.

Were pirates cutthroat criminals bent on theft and murder? Or were they romantic free spirits rebelling against tyrannical military captains and a hopelessly uptight society? The answer is probably a little of each. You might also be interested to know that some pirates really did have peg legs and pet parrots, but walking the plank is a Hollywood invention.

★ ★ ★ ★ ★ ★ ★ ★ ★ ★ ★ ★ ★ ★ ★ ★ ★ ★

Anne skedaddled. The pair slipped away to the captain's ship and headed for the Cat's Cove hideout in the Bahamas.

Captain Jack must've had a fondness for females. Once Anne climbed aboard, his ship, the *Revenge,* was home to the only two women pirates in the Bahamas (at least the only two we know about). On board, Anne met Mary Read, also an illegitimate child with a shady past. So that her mother could inherit money (sons and grandsons inherited, but not female offspring), Mary had been passed off as a boy named Mark. As a youth, she signed on as an English sailor. During a raid by Captain Jack's crew, she was captured—and with them she willingly stayed.

Anne, like Mary, fit right in with the hard-boiled pirate crew. Before long she was climbing the rigging, setting the sails, and keeping a lookout for sandbars and for ships that might make likely prey. On most days, Anne dressed like a woman. When action loomed, however, she hustled to the cramped captain's quarters to grab her sword and pistol and don fighting duds—jacket, trousers, and a silk handkerchief around her head.

The brilliant blue waters of the Bahamas were rife with pirates and privateers. Hundreds of inlets linked 700 lush, tropical islands. Getting around wasn't easy, given the perilous seas. During hurricane season, timbers cracked, winds roared, waves crashed, and thunder boomed. Despite these hazards the sun, moon, stars, shiny brass tools, various charts, and an experienced crew kept the vessel afloat.

When Anne sighted one of the trading ships on its way to Spain, laden with South American gold and silver, she helped the crew heave the sails high. Some ships, trying to lighten their load and outrun the *Revenge,* dumped their cargoes overboard. Games

ANNE AND HER SHIPMATE MARY READ REIGNED AS THE PIRATE QUEENS OF THE BAHAMAS.

of cat and mouse could last for days. Sometimes, the *Revenge* used stealth instead of speed. The crew disguised the ship as a whaler or flew the pursued ship's own flag until the last minute. Then once the ship was in range, the buccaneers hoisted the Jolly Roger flag with its feared black and white skull and fired a shot across the other ship's bow. If the enemy surrendered right away, the *Revenge* seized the ship's goods and marooned the crew on the nearest island.

If the enemy fought back, however, things got dicey. With their great guns (cannons) and pistols, the pirates tried to disable the enemy's mast and board its ship. Sunken treasures, after all, were worth nothing!

Of course, life on board a pirate ship could be bleak and boring, too. Anne shared the 100-foot-long vessel with rats, roaches,

★ ★ ★ ★ ★ ★ ★ ★ ★ ★ ★ ★ ★ ★ ★ ★

and hundreds of men. Sea chests served as dining tables—and gaming tables. Over endless hands of poker, she downed tankards of ale. Like the other pirates, she shared equally in any booty. Her only privilege was not having to stretch a hammock on the deck to sleep, for she shared Calico Jack's captain's quarters.

In 1717 the British decided to make the seas safe for trade again. In a crafty move, they appointed a former pirate, Woodes Rogers, to be the governor of the Bahamas. He offered royal pardons to all who gave up pirating, then blocked the New Providence harbor so that pirates in port could not escape. The landlocked pirates set one of their own ships on fire and sailed it toward the English ships, but in the end, Rogers captured the island.

Calico Jack and the *Revenge* managed to escape capture until 1720, but the pirate business just wasn't what it used to be. Too many British soldiers patrolled the waterways; too many pirates had gone respectable—or had been caught and hanged. The discouraged *Revenge* crew was anchored near Serpent's Mouth drowning their sorrows below deck, when the end came. Too late, a befuddled mate manning the watch spotted a huge royal sloop laden with cannons and smashers (smaller guns for short-range targets) bearing down on the *Revenge:* "God's blood," the mate bellowed. "Yonder be the King's men!"

The *Revenge* lifted its anchor, hoisted the sails, and tore away. However, the contrary wind suddenly died to a whisper, taking the wind right out of weary Captain Rackam's sails, too. When the English boarded the ship, Calico Jack surrendered. Only a few put up valiant fight, including Anne Bonny and Mary Read. As she struggled in vain with the British soldiers, Anne reportedly berated her pitiful mates, "There's not a real man among ye!"

The Court of Admiralty in Jamaica sentenced Jack and his men to be hanged on Gallows Point at Point Royal. When Anne's turn came to face the judge, she stood with her small, calloused hands folded on her belly. "Mistress Bonny, you are a wicked, lustful, thieving, swearing, wench best suited for the gallows. Is there any reason why you should not swing?" the judge thundered. "My Lord," Anne replied saucily, "I Plead my Belly." The scowling judge had no choice but to postpone sentencing, as was the custom of the day. Mary Read also claimed to be pregnant, and both women were returned to prison to await their children's births.

In prison, Mary Read caught a fever and died—and Anne Bonny disappeared without a trace! No record of her release, sentencing, or execution has ever been found.

Legends about Anne Bonny's postprison life abound, of course. Some say a forgiving husband took her back, others that pirate pals busted her out of prison. Some say she repented and got herself to a nunnery; others that she married a rich planter and became a respectable wife. My personal favorite is the story that Anne escaped, fled the colony, took a new name, opened a tavern, and made a fortune. Somehow, that sounds like a fitting fate for wanton wench of the sea!

★ ★ ★ ★ ★ ★ ★ ★ ★ ★ ★ ★ ★ ★ ★ ★ ★ ★

★ ★ ★ ★ ★ ★ ★ ★ ★ ★

Eliza Lucas Pinckney

(1 7 2 2 – 1 7 9 3)

In the Caribbean island of Antigua (pronounced Anteega) little Eliza Lucas smoothed her silken skirts and stirred her English tea with a dainty silver spoon. A house slave brought the steaming beverage to the royal governor's daughter, who against all odds was to become one of the most important planters of colonial South Carolina.

Born in 1722, Eliza was raised on the family's Caribbean plantation and educated in an elite London finishing school. There she learned the "womanly arts" of embroidery, flower arranging, harpsichord playing, and botany. Eliza loved music and played the harpsichord every day of her life, and she did passable embroidery. The subject that really captured her heart, however, was botany, the study of plants. From a young age, Eliza had been drawn to the greenhouses, the barns, the fields, and weighty volumes on growing and breeding plants. At a young age she told her father, "I love the vegetable world immensely!"

★ ★ ★ ★ ★ ★ ★ ★ ★ ★ ★ ★ ★ ★ ★ ★ ★ ★

When Eliza was 15, her family inherited three rice plantations in South Carolina. Soon, 1500-acre Garden Hill plantation,
17 miles from Charleston, became her new home. If Eliza had
been the typical South Carolina belle, she'd have spent many days
and nights shopping and attending parties in the capitol city of
Charleston.

But Eliza wasn't typical and, as luck would have it, a brouhaha
caused by a British sea captain named Robert Jenkins intervened.
Jenkins claimed that Spaniards of Florida had boarded his ship in
the Atlantic and had cut off his ear. Some say Jenkins actually cut
off his own ear to stir things up (he carried it around in a little box!).
Either way, however, the episode (and a lot of tension over trade
routes) started a war between England and Spain, which came to
be known as the War of Jenkins Ear. Eliza's father returned to Antigua to join the fight.

Did Eliza's father hire an overseer to run the three vast plantations? Did he hire a housekeeper to care for his invalid wife (who
died a year later) and his children? No! Mr. Lucas was confident
that his dark-eyed daughter could manage the family, the plantations, the slaves, and the servants. She could grow rice, collect
pitch from trees, harvest the wood lots, raise the livestock, and su-
pervise hundreds of servants and slaves. Eliza had proven from a
young age that she could do anything she set her mind to.

As it turned out, Eliza loved her new responsibilities. In the
evenings, by dim candlelight, she swept back her chestnut curls
and wrote to her father about every detail of her busy life. At dawn,
Eliza rose to the sound of a conch shell being blown to summon
the slave gang to the fields. Then, before breakfast, she read for
two hours, walked in the garden, and gave the servants their or-

ders. After grabbing a quick bite, Eliza then played music and studied shorthand, French, and law. In the afternoon she knuckled down to plantation business, then taught two slaves girls to read and write. (In the South at that time, only 1 percent of male and female slaves could read, so this practice was unusual for a plantation mistress.) After dinner, Eliza tried to get in a little needlework. Even then, however, peace was hard to come by. Neighbors who couldn't afford to hire a lawyer often stopped by to ask the most learned woman in the countryside for help writing their wills and business contracts.

Not all of Eliza's neighbors approved of her status as a learned lady, of course. "She will damage her health with such manly behavior," her critics gossiped. One gentlewoman confronted Eliza directly. "Mistress Lucas, you'll go crazy as a June bug in May if you don't rest your poor little brain!" she scolded. Then Eliza's nosy neighbor grabbed Eliza's volume of *Plutarch's Lives* and tried to throw it in the fire!

The more Eliza managed plantation business affairs, the more competent she became. When she realized that conflicts between England and the colonies were creating a shortage of goods, she got busy trying to remedy that. "South Carolina must become more self-sufficient," she said. "I'm going to discover which crops will grow best in our soil and climate." With an inventor's passion, Eliza began her experiments. She planted trial plots of figs, ginger, hemp, flax, cotton, alfalfa, silk, cotton, and indigo.

Meanwhile, Eliza's father was planning his daughter's future from afar. To please society, Eliza attended some highbrow parties in Charleston once in a while. To her father's dismay, however, she preferred plants to suitors. "When it comes to the other sex," she told her father in letters, "I can't be bothered right now." By the time Eliza was 22—back then that was getting up in years!—Eliza's father had begun to worry. He decided it was high time she married, so he selected a suitable planter for her. Well! That didn't sit well with independent Eliza! "I don't respect that man," she wrote. "All the riches of Peru and Chile cannot make me marry him!" In the face of such passion, Eliza's doting daddy gave in and let Eliza choose her own mate. In 1743, she married a longtime friend, Charles Pinckney.

Pinckney, a 44-year-old widower, was a very rich lawyer, politician, and planter. He was also South Carolina's attorney general, speaker of its House of Commons, and a judge. Because he was so swamped, guess who began managing his seven plantations and his waterfront mansion in Charleston? Right—Eliza! Along

LOVE SOUTHERN STYLE

Eliza Pinckney had married a man twice her age. That was common among aristocratic southerners because it was a good way to build wealth and power. "Good marriages" joined land and fortunes. If love happened, the newlyweds were just plain lucky. Parents usually picked spouses (stubborn daughters like Eliza were exceptions to the rule), and those who rebelled often became outcasts. In fact, couples who eloped were sometimes jailed! In the south, marriage was also forever—no matter what. Divorce was unheard of, even if there was abuse or neglect.

★ ★ ★ ★ ★ ★ ★ ★ ★ ★ ★ ★ ★ ★ ★ ★ ★ ★

the way, she also found time to give birth to two sons and a daughter—Charles, Thomas, and Harriot.

Motherhood now competed with agriculture in Eliza's heart and mind. From Europe, she imported the latest books on child rearing and pored over them. In fact, Eliza's intellectual curiosity and zest for life shone through everything she did. When someone asked her why she rose so early and went to bed so late, she said, "The longer we are awake, the longer we live. The more we sleep, the more we lose of life."

Along with her husband's plantations, Eliza continued to manage her father's. On this vast acreage, she added fields of flax and hemp. She also focused her attention on growing indigo, a plant used for making a valuable deep blue fabric dye. By 1745, Eliza finally had her bumper crop. With great excitement, she set about establishing a booming new industry for the colony. For that,

★ ★ ★ ★ ★ ★ ★ ★ ★ ★ ★ ★ ★ ★ ★ ★ ★ ★

she had to get other planters involved, so Eliza sent indigo seeds to planters all over South Carolina. In a few years, the gold-leafed indigo had taken off like wildfire. By 1750, it was the south's second most important cash crop. In fact, the French (who grew lots of indigo, too) were so irritated by the competition that they passed a new law. Anyone in France caught exporting indigo seed got the death penalty!

After Eliza's husband grew ill and died in 1757, she raised her children and continued managing her empire. During the American Revolution, she and her children sided with the Rebels. As a result, two of Eliza's plantations were burned to ashes. Many of her slaves ran away, too, taking advantage of a British offer to free slaves who left their owners and sided with the British. Despite these setbacks, Eliza didn't give up. After the war, she rebuilt her agricultural empire from the ground up.

In 1791, President George Washington toured the south to win support for the new national government. He and his entourage stopped to visit Eliza Pinckney's Hampton Plantation. Washington was impressed with Eliza's vast knowledge of farming—and the awesome breakfast she served. In his diary, Washington gushed about Eliza's plentiful servings of juicy meat pies and sweet pastries!

Two years after Washington's visit, in 1793 (at age 71), Eliza had lost her normal vim and vigor. No longer could she pack a wallop into every single day. Determined to find a cure, Eliza traveled to Philadelphia to see a specialist. The very next day, she died of advanced cancer. At his own request, President George Washington helped carry her coffin to St. Peter's Church graveyard.

★ ★ ★ ★ ★ ★ ★ ★ ★ ★ ★

Anne Trotter Bailey

(1 7 4 3 – 1 8 2 5)

I n the spring of 1775, a 32-year-old widow named Anne Hen-
nis Trotter (sometimes spelled Ann) donned a buckskin jacket,
tucked a tomahawk into her belt, and hefted a musket. She
stepped out of her log cabin in western Virginia and mounted her horse named Liverpool (after her English hometown). She
rode west into the towering Appalachians to
be a frontier scout—and didn't look back.

Little is known of Anne's life before
age 19, when she left a slum in Liverpool for
Staunton, Virginia, in the Shenandoah Valley. In exchange for her passage to Virginia,
she agreed to work as an indentured servant
for four years on a farm. Although she was
English, Anne soon felt she belonged to the
hardy clan of Presbyterian Scots in the val-

★ ★ ★ ★ ★ ★ ★ ★ ★ ★ ★ ★ ★ ★ ★ ★ ★ ★ ★

ley. She milked cows, stoked fires, threshed wheat, spun flax, and learned to shoot the mountain lions and wolves that killed the farmers' livestock.

In 1761, when Anne arrived in the Shenandoah Valley, her master, Joseph Bell, was fighting for the British in the French and Indian War in the Ohio River valley. Both the French and the British desperately wanted to control the vast wilderness beyond the colonies' western mountains. (Most western tribes allied themselves with the French because they were serious fur traders. In contrast the English colonists were into creating farms and building towns.)

Two years later, the British had defeated France, and the valley people rejoiced, especially because many colonial veterans received a small plot of wilderness land for their service. However, King George II, quickly made it known that he wanted no more trouble with western tribes. In the official Proclamation of 1763, he commanded, "I forbid my subjects to settle west of the Appalachians."

Anne, like other valley folks, really resented the king's command that they not head west. Richard Trotter, a French and Indian war veteran and Anne's beau, was upset, too. He and Anne talked things over and decided to defy the king. When Anne's term of service was up, they married and traveled a hundred miles southwest of the Bell's farm (near modern-day Covington) to stake their hilltop claim.

By venturing west of the Shenandoah Valley, Anne and Richard angered the Shawnee, as well as the king. The Cherokee and Iroquois had signed a treaty giving up their claim to western mountains—but the powerful Shawnee had not. Horrified by the people trespassing on their lands, the Shawnee launched attacks on isolated settlements west of Richard and Anne's. To protect the frontier, Richard signed up to work as a scout. He kept tabs on Shawnee activity and reported to militia commanders at a string of remote frontier forts.

Meanwhile, Anne and their young son, William, were left to fend for themselves. Isolation in the wilderness did odd things to people. Some went crazy; others scurried back to civilization. Anne got a little wild and woolly. While other women gathered to gab about births, deaths, love, and marriage on the frontier post, Anne

★ ★ ★ ★ ★ ★ ★ ★ ★ ★ ★ ★ ★ ★ ★ ★ ★ ★

SOUL DRIVERS

Becoming an indentured servant in colonial America was a gamble. Some had kind masters, and the gamble paid off. Others, however, had cruel masters who overworked, beat, and starved them. Each indentured servant signed a contract promising to work for 4 to 10 years in exchange for free passage to America, food, clothing, and roofs over their heads. If servants disobeyed, masters could add years to their contract. Newspapers were filled with advertisements looking for runaway indentured servants.

If being an indentured servant was a gamble, the alternative was worse. In Britain and Europe, high rents, overcrowding, famine, and a rigid system of social classes kept millions in poverty. In eighteenth–century London, things were so bad that the city hired women to gather abandoned babies left on the streets and to take them to workhouses. Only a tenth of these babies survived past infancy. America offered the European poor their only hope for a better life, so agents called "soul drivers" had no problem finding recruits. In the early colonial years, half of all immigrants to America came as indentured servants.

★ ★ ★ ★ ★ ★ ★ ★ ★ ★ ★ ★ ★ ★ ★ ★ ★ ★

hobnobbed with menfolk at the tavern. She debated county politics, bet on fighting roosters, and downed home-brewed whiskey. Anne's shenanigans caused some tongues to cluck, but most of her neighbors didn't mind her odd ways one bit. "The Tidewater gentry can have their fancy do's and don'ts," the mountain people said. "Here, folks do as they please."

While Anne lived life on her own terms and Richard fought the Shawnee, rebellion brewed to the east and west. Colonials and British clashed and boycotts raged in the east. In 1774, Lord Dunmore, the Royal Governor of Virginia and New York, promised to lead Redcoats to Point Pleasant on the Ohio, where they'd meet a thousand Virginians and "end the Indian Problem." Dunmore and the Redcoats never arrived, however, so the Virginians fought a large Shawnee army alone. After the smoke cleared from the bloody battle, Richard Trotter was among the dead.

When Anne learned of her young husband's death, she became a little unhinged. In the dead of winter, she holed up in a cave behind the 40-foot Falling Springs waterfall. Neighbors followed Liverpool's trail to the cave and brought Anne safely home. By spring, she was healthy and sane again—yet changed forever. To her neighbors' surprise, she threw off her linsey-woolsey gown and donned Richard's buckskin, then she left her son with a neighbor and took Richard's place scouting on the frontier.

From spring through fall, Anne delivered guns, ammunition, messages, and medical supplies among a string of wilderness forts that protected settlers from attacks. Guided by a pocket compass, Anne rode along high rocky Allegheny ridges and through deep canyons. She carved dugout canoes from tree trunks to cross the rivers, scaled steep hillsides, bedded down in hollow tree trunks.

She could throw a hunting knife straight at a mark and could load her musket rifle on the run. When people asked how she managed on her own, Anne jutted out her round chin and said, "I can ride, hunt, and chop as well as any a man!" When they asked, "Do Indians ever try to kill you?" Anne replied that Native Americans thought the Great Spirit protected her, so they left her alone. Besides, she said, "I could only be killed, and everyone has to die sometime."

Once, Anne was at Fort Lee in Charleston when hostile Shawnee arrived and camped across the river. Fearing an attack, everyone inside prepared for a siege. They shooed the small children into lofts and picked up their guns. After a soldier discovered the gunpowder barrel was almost empty, fear spread through the fort. Anne volunteered to fetch powder from the nearest fort in Lewisburg, 100 miles away. At nightfall, she mounted Liverpool, slipped out the gate, and galloped through moonlit woods. After two days and two nights, she reached Fort Savannah in Lewisburg. There, she loaded gunpowder into sacks, rested briefly, and returned to Fort Lee. The settlers inside cheered as Anne arrived with the powder needed to stave off attacks.

Although the British surrendered in 1781, the Shawnee and allied tribes didn't let up for another decade. During those years, Anne continued scouting with her new husband and fellow scout, John Bailey. By the late 1790s, however, John had grown ill and died, and the frontier had shifted west of the Mississippi. Wagons, carts, and herds of livestock now rumbled along the Midland Trail from Staunton, Virginia, to the Ohio River. Anne was part of a dying breed, but she wasn't ready for the rocking chair! To continue her gypsy life, she took to peddling. From the east, she brought spinning wheels, pocketknives, and gaggles of geese for the growing commu-

nities. She was, by all accounts, honest to a cent, yet clever as a fox.

One day, Captain William Clendenin, who had turned Fort Lee into his home, asked Anne to drive 20 geese to his house. "Anne, if you don't fetch exactly 20 geese, I will not pay for any," the shrewd old captain said. Anne agreed, then drove the geese 60 miles to Clendenin's home. When Anne arrived, she told him one goose had died on the trip. "Well, Anne," the captain said gleefully. "You didn't bring the number promised, so I cannot pay for them." Anne walked out to where she had hitched her horse, took the dead goose from her bag, and threw it down in the yard. "There's your 20," she said, with fire in her eyes. Captain Clendenin laughed and promptly paid up. Then he invited Anne into the house for a bite to eat.

In 1818, Anne was 75 and finally ready to settle down. Her son William lived with his wife and two daughters across the Ohio River. Anne moved to be near her family, yet insisted on building her own rough log cabin made out of split rails used for fences. Not long before her death in 1825, a roving journalist named Anne Royall told the scout's story. After Anne Bailey's death, poets sang her praises. In 1928, Anne Sharkey called Anne the "original Girl Scout."

★ ★ ★ ★ ★ ★ ★ ★ ★ ★

Mary Draper Ingles

(1 7 3 1   —   1 8 1 5)

For hundreds of years, Mary Draper Ingles's lowland Scottish ancestors wielded swords and pikes to defend various Protestant monarchs fighting against Catholic armies. Unfortunately, the victorious Protestant kings and queens were hardly grateful. Instead, the Anglicans booted the Scots to Ireland, where they faced hostile Catholics, worn out soil, and famine. Newlyweds George and Eleanor Draper—like hundreds of thousands of their fellow Scotch-Irish—finally had enough and headed for the New World. In 1729, the newlyweds landed in Philadelphia, where their first daughter, Mary, was born.

When Mary was a child, her family traveled south on the Great Wagon Road to the Shenandoah Valley of Virginia. then when she was 15, they settled farther west, in the fertile Appalachians.

The Drapers headed a pack of Germans and Scotch-Irish Presbyterian immigrants who peopled the mountains. As in England, Virginia's official religion was Anglican. West of the Blue Ridge Mountains, however, Virginia officials let the Scotch-Irish

★ ★ ★ ★ ★ ★ ★ ★ ★ ★ ★ ★ ★ ★ ★ ★ ★ ★

Presbyterians practice their faith freely. The easterners of Tidewater, Virginia, knew the Scotch-Irish would make excellent border guards to protect the more settled eastern region. A border guard's life can be dangerous, but the Drapers had waited centuries to own their own ground. If risk of danger was the price to be paid, they'd pay it courageously. "I'll die before any man—red or white—chases me from this land," Mary's father swore.

A small, windowless log cabin near the churning New River became the Drapers' home. Mary's father, George, strapped himself into a simple iron plow. John, Mary's only sibling, held the handles while the blade turned over the black soil. Mary and Eleanor,

her mother, walked behind, dropping kernels of corn in rows. Before long, a small village called Draper's Meadow sprang up. The community's crops grew tall and hardy—and so did Mary.

Often the Drapers worked side by side with their neighbors, including widower Thomas Ingles and his three sons. On summer evenings, Mary ran as fleet-footed as the boys during games of "Fox and Geese." The Draper's Meadow folks laughed and said of the tall, lanky girl with the flyaway hair, "She's as tough as a boy, but she'll settle down once she's married." After Mary's father disappeared while out hunting, her willowy strength was needed more than ever. A search turned up no body, but George Draper was presumed dead—killed by a bear, a rattler, or perhaps hostile warriors. A weaker family might have hightailed it back to civilization when the man of the family died, but Eleanor Draper and her children stayed put, holding tight to the family land.

In 1750, 19-year-old Mary married Thomas Ingles's son, 20-year-old Will. In five years, the couple had two sons, Thomas and George. After Mary's brother John married a girl named Bettie, the newlyweds moved next door. Mary now cooked, cleaned, watched the children, and helped with the harvest, while Will farmed and hunted. When decisions were to be made, Mary spoke her mind freely, and Will listened.

In the mid-1750s, bands of French-allied Shawnee began raiding the western Virginia frontier. Growing white settlements were driving away game and disrupting the native fur trade. The French, who also claimed the Ohio River valley, were arming the natives. Like most frontier colonists, Mary had little sympathy for Native Americans and believed they wasted good land by not turning all the forests into fields.

In the fall of 1755, Will Ingles and John Draper headed to the fields to harvest the wheat. Mary was hugely pregnant with her third child, Bettie was nursing her new baby girl, and Mary's mother, Eleanor, was watching the boys play in the clearing. Bettie's baby slept peacefully in a hollowed-log cradle. None of the women dreamed that their first major challenge as border guards was about to commence—what a trial it would be.

Suddenly, from inside her cabin, Mary heard Bettie scream. Mary ran to the door to see Bettie, shot in the arm, crouching next to her dead baby. Across the yard, a Shawnee warrior stood over Eleanor's lifeless body—and another stood over Mary's sobbing sons, Georgie, 2, and Thomas, 4. Mary, herded into a huddle with

★ ★ ★ ★ ★ ★ ★ ★ ★ ★ ★ ★ ★ ★ ★ ★ ★ ★

THE GREAT WAGON ROAD

At one time, the Great Warrior's Trail leading from Philadelphia to the Carolinas was the highway of the powerful Iroquois Confederation, comprising the Seneca, Mohawk, Onondaga, Oneida, Tuscarora, and Cayuga nations. In 1722, however, the six nations gave up their claim to their hunting grounds from the Blue Ridge to the Mississippi River. Although the Shawnee still claimed the area, the door was cracked open to settlement.

Private landowners and local governments used laborers and indentured servants to grub out trees and brush on either side of the narrow trail, which soon was dubbed the Great Wagon Road. The rutted dirt road—which ran through central Pennsylvania, then south through the Great Shenandoah Valley into the Carolina mountains—saw more traffic than all the other colonial roads put together.

★ ★ ★ ★ ★ ★ ★ ★ ★ ★ ★ ★ ★ ★ ★ ★ ★ ★

the rest of the captives, watched helplessly as the warriors set Draper's Meadow on fire.

Mary didn't know it, but the warriors were launching the first raids of the seven-year French and Indian War. They hustled the captives now including Mary and Bettie, toward the woods. Mary and her children rode a stolen horse. Bettie, forced to walk, stumbled along, clutching her bleeding arm. Mary prayed that Will and John were safe and would rescue them. Such a rescue seemed impossible, though as the natives had taken all the horses, and the nearest settlement was many miles away.

All her life, Mary had heard about warriors taking captives. Some captives were killed to exact revenge, or sold as slaves, or adopted. Mary prayed for strength and ordered her children to stop whimpering. "We must show no weakness or they will kill us," she told her boys urgently. "Be strong, Bettie," she called to her sister-in-law.

Days later, on a leafy woodland floor, Mary gave birth to a baby girl. Afterward, the warriors motioned for Mary to pick up her baby and get back on her horse. Mary did, for otherwise she thought they'd be killed. As she grew stronger again, Mary fixed food for the party, and she bathed Bettie's wound. The Shawnee saw Mary as the captives' leader and admired her above the others.

The lower New River (now called the Kanawha) at last dumped into a wide body of blue-green water called the O-yo-o (Ohio).

For several days, the group followed the river and used hidden canoes to cross smaller rivers that fed it. A few weeks later, the group glided up the Scotio River until they reached a town of neat houses and fields. A throng of men, women, children, and wolf-like dogs appeared and yanked out the captives. When the mob pinched, slapped, spit, and hissed at them, Mary ordered her boys not to cry.

In the center of the village, the Shawnee tied the captives to poles, where several other whites recently captured in Pennsylvania already cowered. In the square, the huddled captives whispered to each other, as a double line of Shawnee men, women, and children formed. It looked as if they were about to dance the Virginia Reel, but their fists clutched sticks and bramble switches. An old German woman whispered to the other captives that they would soon have to run the gauntlet. "If you make it to the end, you live. If you don't, you die." Most of the adult captives took turns running through the two lines as heavy blows rained down on their legs and back. The Shawnee so admired Mary, however, that she was spared the ordeal.

In the coming days, worse trials followed. Mary's sons and Bettie were adopted into Shawnee families and were taken to distant villages. Mary waited for her daughter to be taken, but again she was favored. In a great council circle, a Shawnee warrior acted out Mary's fortitude and leadership on the trail. Then a young native woman led both her and her baby to a vacant hut.

In early October, Mary and the German captive were taken on a salt-making expedition. The party included several warriors, two French fur traders, a few Shawnee women, Mary, and the German woman. In canoes, they traveled 150 miles downriver before pulling into the swampy ground where salt would be extracted.

Back in the village, Mary and the German woman had been watched carefully, but during the salt-making trip, the Shawnee let the two women roam freely. The Shawnee and the Frenchmen thought the women would never dream of trying to escape from such a remote place—but they were wrong! Mary longed for home and could tolerate it no longer. This was her one chance to escape, and she would take it!

After several days at the salt-making camp, Mary announced her plan to the old German woman, whose name she could not understand. "Will you go with me?" she asked the German woman. Horrified, the old woman answered, "No, no, Mary Ingles. Winter is coming and we will starve!" But Mary's mind was fixed on freedom.

Mary told the older woman she would leave her daughter behind, for the infant would never survive. Her only hope was to get home and try to ransom her children. Finally the German woman agreed. One day, they went to gather food, walked north along the Ohio River—and didn't look back.

On their long journey home, Mary and the old German woman passed through the wildest country east of the Mississippi. Traveling with Shawnee hunters was a far cry from going it alone on foot. Wide rivers poured into the Ohio, blocking their path. The hidden canoes had rotted or had washed away in floods. Neither woman could swim, so they had to hike up the tributaries until the water was shallow enough to wade across. At night, the women burrowed inside piles of leaves. For added warmth, they snuggled close.

After a few days, the stolen corn was gone. Foraging only netted a few dried grapes and nuts, and the older woman grumbled nonstop about her empty belly. Mary had almost given up hope when they arrived at the Kanawha River which led to her home. Knowing she'd never find her way on the twisted paths, Mary stuck with her plan to follow the river. She headed into the razorback ridges of the New River valley—country even the natives hadn't seen before! Mary and the old woman scrambled up cliffs, hiked on ledges, and crawled through mountain laurel thickets. They tripped over forest debris washed off the steep slopes during storms. Briars and brambles tore their dresses to shreds. Black and blue bruises and crusted blood disfigured their swollen feet.

It was November by then, and light snow sometimes covered the ground. Crazed with hunger, the old woman grabbed roots from Mary's hands and screamed at her. Then the old woman cracked and lunged at Mary with her tomahawk. "I'm going to eat you May-re Ink-les," she screamed. Mary fought her off and stumbled up the New River alone.

Luck was with Mary, for she discovered a canoe in the weeds, crossed the New River, and found two old turnips in an abandoned garden. Later, she said they were the best meal of her life! Home was only 30 miles away, but Mary could no longer feel her feet or see straight. Still, she dragged one foot in front of the other. On the second day after eating the turnips, Mary came to a sheer, 300-foot cliff. The rock face had no ledges, shelving rocks, or footholds—only small saplings and bushes growing from crevices. There was no way around, so she climbed up, using saplings and shrubs like the rungs of a ladder. It took her nearly all day—later, a day she called the most terrible one of her life.

When Mary reached the summit, she rolled down the other side and saw a miracle: a field of corn and a hunting cabin! On all fours, like a wounded animal, Mary crawled her scratched body

through the tall stalks. "Help! Help!" she cried. Mary's neighbor, Adam Harman, gaped at the nearly naked skeleton with stark white hair, then rushed to carry her inside. As he picked her up, Adam looked closely and gasped, "Surely that can't be you, Mary Ingles!?"

Adam Harman wrapped Mary in blankets, killed a calf to make some healing beef soup, and bathed her frostbitten feet. Mary told of her grueling 42-day, 800-mile journey home, and learned that her husband had gone to the Ohio River valley to find and ransom the captives. After taking Mary to the Dunkard's

TOWARD THE END OF THEIR LONG TREK HOME, MARY'S COMPANION GOT A BIT LOOPY AND ATTACKED MARY WITH A TOMAHAWK.

★ ★ ★ ★ ★ ★ ★ ★ ★ ★ ★ ★ ★ ★ ★ ★ ★

Bottom Fort, a search party found the German woman. When she tottered into the fort on her bare purple feet, the two women stumbled into a hug and wept. The next day, Mary wept again—with joy and sorrow. Will Ingles returned safely, but without any news of the children or of Bettie.

After Mary's ordeal, you'd think she would choose to leave the mountains forever. Without their land, however, the Ingles family had no wealth, no independence, no life. On the New River, they built a two-story log home and inn, and they operated a ferry. A sturdy palisade fence surrounded the house, which Will and Mary called Fort Hope. Hope, in fact, sustained Mary. Although she bore five more children, she and Will spent years looking for the three who'd been taken by the Shawnee. In 1763, Bettie was ransomed and told the Drapers that Georgie had died, but Thomas was living in a native village near Detroit. Five years later, when Thomas was a teenager, he returned home to his parents.

In 1782, Will died, and in 1815, Mary followed. For generations, her cabin at Draper's Meadow stood vacant; then the roof finally caved in. Many years later, descendants of Mary Draper Ingles tore down the chimney and carted the rocks to Mary Ingles's grave. There they built a monument to their foremother, one of the most remarkable women who ever lived on the colonial frontier.

SUGGESTED READING

★ ★ ★ ★ ★ ★ ★ ★ ★ ★ ★ ★ ★ ★ ★

The following books are recommended for young readers.

Allen, Paula Gunn. *As Long As the Rivers Flow: The Stories of Nine Native Americans.* New York: Scholastic, 1996.

Demos, John. *The Tried and the True: Native American Women Confronting Colonization* (Young Oxford History of Women in the United States, Vol. 1). New York: Oxford University Press, 1998.

Fritz, Jean. *Can't You Make Them Behave, King George?* New York: Paperstar, 1996.

Fritz, Jean. *The Double Life of Pocahontas.* New York: Putnam, 1983.

Furbcc, Mary Rodd. *Anne Bailey: Frontier Scout.* Greensboro, NC: Morgan Reynolds, 2001.

Furbee, Mary Rodd. *Mary Ingles: Indian Captive.* Greensboro, NC: Morgan Reynolds, 2001.

★ ★ ★ ★ ★ ★ ★ ★ ★ ★ ★ ★ ★ ★ ★ ★ ★ ★

Furbee, Mary Rodd. *Nancy Ward: Beloved Woman of the Cherokee.* Greensboro, NC: Morgan Reynolds, 2001.

Furbee, Mary Rodd. *Women of the American Revolution (History Makers).* San Diego, CA: Lucent Books, 1999.

Hakim, Joy. *From Colonies to Country* and *Making Thirteen Colonies (History of U.S., Books 1 & 2).* New York: Oxford University Press Children's Books, 1999.

Kamensky, Jane. *The Colonial Mosaic: American Women 1600–1760 (Young Oxford History of Women in the United States, Vol. 2.)* New York: Oxford University Press, 1995.

King, David C. *Colonial Days: Discover the Past with Fun Projects, Games, Activities, and Recipes* (American Kids in History Series). New York: John Wiley & Sons, Inc., 1997.

Norton, Mary Beth. *Founding Mothers: Women of America in the Revolutionary Era.* Boston: Houghton Mifflin, 1975.

Salmon, Marylynn. *The Limits of Independence: American Women, 1760–1800 (Young Oxford History of Women in the United States, Vol. 3).* New York: Oxford University Press, 1994.

Sherrow, Victoria. *Phyllis Wheatley.* New York: Chelsea House Publishing, 1993.

St. George, Judith. *Betsy Ross: Patriot of Philadelphia.* New York: Henry Holt & Company, 1997.

Wagoner, Jean Brown. *Abigail Adams: Girl of Colonial Days (Childhood of Famous Americans).* Aladdin Paperbacks, 1992.

Wheatherly, Myra. *Women Pirates: Eight Stories of Adventure.* Greensboro, NC: Morgan Reynolds, Inc., 1998.

Zeinert, Karen. *Those Remarkable Women of the American Revolution.* Brookfield, CT: Millbrook Press, 1996.

★ ★ ★ ★ ★ ★ ★ ★ ★ ★ ★ ★ ★ ★ ★ ★ ★ ★

Anne Marbury Hutchinson: 1591–1643

Margaret Brent: 1601–1671

Queen Weetamoo: 163?–1667

Anne Bonny: 1697–17??

Eliza Lucas Pinckney: 1722–1793

Mary Draper Ingles: 1731–1815

Elizabeth "Mumbet" Freeman: 1742–1829

Anne Trotter Bailey: 1743–1825

Abigail Smith Adams: 1744–1818

Esther DeBerdt Reed: 1746–1780

Betsy Griscom Ross: 1752–1836

Phillis Wheatley: 1753–1784

Peggy Shippen Arnold: 1760–1804

Deborah Samson: 1760–1831

If you'd like to know about additional interesting colonial women, check out the following list and browse the Suggested Reading list on p. 113.

- **Mary Musgrove** (Cousaponokeesa) was a Creek interpreter, diplomat, and businesswoman. When the English came to set up the colony of Georgia, they hired Mary to be the colony's interpreter and advisor. After her English husband died in 1735, Mary became the wealthiest woman—Native American or white—on the Georgia frontier. She controlled vast parcels of land, including islands off the Atlantic coast. When fighting broke out between the Spanish and the English, Mary influenced the Creeks to join the British. After Mary's husband died, the British challenged her land ownership. She fought the issue in court and, eventually, won back some of her property.

- **Lady Deborah Dunch Moody** planned, built, and ran her own town of Gravesend, New Netherlands (later Brooklyn, New York). In 1640, this widow of a knighted English lord had risked arrest by the English crown for being too chummy with Puritans (and other "heretics"). So she sewed her fortune in the lining of her gown and her young son's coat, and she headed for the colonies. Once there, she invested wisely, added to her fortune, and built her own tidy little town. Heretics of all stripes were welcome, which made the neighboring Massachusetts Pilgrims declare that Lady Deborah was a "very dangerous woman."

- **Nancy Ward,** whose tribal name was Nanye'hi, was a Beloved Woman of the Cherokee (in present-day North Carolina and Tennessee). After displaying bravery in battle in the 1750s—women could be warriors—Nancy earned her title and became head of the Cherokee Women's Council. In that role, she conducted ceremonies to purify warriors, decided the fate of prisoners, and voted on the tribal council. During treaty negotiations with whites, Nancy sometimes served as a spokesperson for the tribe. Although she befriended white settlers and spoke for peace, she also warned her people not to give up more land.

- **Martha Washington** of Virginia, wife of George Washington, nursed the sick, shared her rations, and comforted the dying at Valley Forge in November of 1777. During eight war-torn years, Martha ran a large plantation—Mount Vernon—alone. During the winters, she joined her husband in camp. Martha agonized secretly and profoundly over the suffering caused by war and greatly feared the constant threat to her husband's life.

★ ★ ★ ★ ★ ★ ★ ★ ★ ★ ★ ★ ★ ★ ★ ★ ★ ★

CREDITS

★ ★ ★ ★ ★ ★ ★ ★

Image of King Philip of the Wampanoags (p. 17): Anne S. K. Brown Military Collection, Brown University Library

Portrait of Elizabeth "Mumbet" Freeman (p. 31): courtesy of the Massachusetts Historical Society

Portrait of Abigail Adams (p. 35): courtesy of the Massachusetts Historical Society

"A View of the Town of Boston in New England" (p. 36): Print Collection, Miriam and Ira D. Wallach Division of Art, Prints and Photographs, the New York Public Library, Astor, Lenox and Tilden Foundations

Image of Phyllis Wheatley (p. 45): courtesy of the Massachusetts Historical Society

Image of Margaret Brent Before the Court (p. 58): Louis Glanzman/National Geographic Society Image Collection

Portrait of Esther Reed (p. 76): courtesy of the Frick Art Reference Library

Image of "Ladies Working for Washington" (p. 80): Bettmann/Corbis

Image of Mulberry Plantation (House and Street) (p. 93): Gibbes Museum of Art/Carolina Art Association

Image of "Woman in Front of Log Cabin" (p. 104): courtesy of the Library of Congress